'Can you write that in a Christian book, darling?'
Mum

'Once in a while, a new voice comes along, someone who really has something to say. In a world of well-meaning advice about love and relationships, Lauren is like that trusted friend who tells you the whole truth and nothing but the truth – and you'll love her for it. *Notes on Love* is kind, thoughtful, wise and pretty much relentlessly hilarious – there's a decent joke on almost every page. Everyone needs a friend like Lauren.'
Martin Saunders, author, Director of Innovation, Youthscape, and Director, Satellites

'Beautiful read! The topic of singleness in the Church is one that's not often talked about and, when it is, it is often from a view of incompleteness and inferiority. This needs to change. Lauren talks about this topic with the seriousness it deserves, with humour sprinkled throughout. Her tips, anecdotes, research, call for a better "way to community" and prayers are a wonderful addition. I wish someone had given me this book as a reminder to enjoy every season in life and not miss the beauty in it all.'
Corina Straub, photographer and Editor of *Chapel*

'Raw, hilarious and painfully observant, this impassioned plea to treat single people as people should be required reading for all Christians. Full of stories and research, *Notes on Love* will reshape its readers' perceptions and, hopefully – let's dream big – the Church. Lauren, you are a star and I can't begin to understand why you are single (as I might have said before reading your book).'
Jo Swinney, author and speaker

'Lauren's book was an amazing read – full of honesty, with a realness to it. I used to read a fair few dating books growing up but most of them shamed me in my thinking. I wish I had had this book back then! It is written in a non-judgemental, honest way, and you will laugh, cry, feel a sense of relief and gain so much from this book. I will definitely be recommending this to people!'
Hope Virgo, multi-award-winning mental health campaigner and author

T0317230

Lauren Windle is a public speaker and journalist, published by Mail Online, *Huffington Post*, *The Sun*, Fabulous Digital, *Marie Claire*, *The Star*, *Church Times* and others. On 22 April 2014 she got clean and sober from a cocaine and alcohol addiction and became a Christian five days later. She has a Master's in Addiction Studies, runs a charity recovery course for people struggling with addiction and, in 2018, gave a TEDx Talk about her personal story of addiction and recovery. She is also the proud owner of a Blue Peter badge and has her grade four ice-skating. You can connect with Lauren @_lauren_celeste on Instagram and Twitter.

NOTES ON LOVE

Being single and dating in a
marriage-obsessed Church

Lauren Windle

First published in Great Britain in 2021

Society for Promoting Christian Knowledge
36 Causton Street
London SW1P 4ST
www.spck.org.uk

British Library Cataloguing-in-Publication Data
A catalogue record for this book is available from the British Library

ISBN 978–0–281–08555–2
eBook ISBN 978–0–281–08556–9

1 3 5 7 9 10 8 6 4 2

Typeset by Fakenham Prepress Solutions, Fakenham, Norfolk NR21 8NL
First printed in Great Britain by Jellyfish Print Solutions

eBook by Fakenham Prepress Solutions, Fakenham, Norfolk NR21 8NL

Produced on paper from sustainable forests

For Leo and Winnie
It's not possible for two people to be more loved.

Contents

Contents

Part 3
TRUE LOVE

Not another Christian dating book

'Christians say stupid things.'

Bella sipped her Turkish coffee while I choked back a laugh of agreement. She's right, they really do. She reeled off the stock phrases she's been 'encouraged' with over her years of being single in the Church: 'God knows best', 'You must be being picky', 'Be patient'.

When surveying the societal 'checklist' of desirable attributes, Bella undoubtedly fares well: articulate, thoughtful, talented, slim, beautiful, with shampoo-advert-shiny hair. The fact is, 'ticking boxes' doesn't make it easier to find the right partner. There are plenty of ugly, boring people who are married.

'When I talk about this, why does some middle-aged, happily married church leader always feel the need to give me a reason for it?' We sat in a coffee shop in Piccadilly while I plied her with questions about her experiences of dating in the Church, in exchange for a cream tea. 'When did the Church lose its ability to just sit with people? To weep with those who weep? Why does everyone have to have an answer for everything?'

I nodded. She's right again. My experience of Christian 'encouragement' over the years is that it's often poorly judged and liberally applied. I crammed half a scone into my mouth (cream then jam – thanks for asking) and offered her silence, in the hope she would extend her insightful monologue to fill it.

'I just want someone in the Church to say, "That must be really painful for you. I don't know what to say." I mean, why can't they admit that some things in life are just shit and we don't know why?!' Bella, between bites of her scone and jokes about dating apps, expressed a view I've heard countless times in the last few months: we're getting this wrong. The narrative around dating and being single is restrictive, anxiety-inducing and pressurized, and those who aren't single either don't think the problem exists or don't know how to fix it. More dangerously, perhaps, many are addressing being single as if it is the problem itself.

1

Since I became Christian seven years ago, the message I've understood from the Church on dating is as follows: marriage is best. Find someone and get married before you're 30. Don't be desperate. Don't shag anyone.

For those who are brave enough to admit to struggling with any or all of these notions, there is an abundance of 'solutions' and a tired 'encouraging' rhetoric: patience, prayer and God's plan. It's potentially all accurate; it's probably all familiar; it's definitely not helpful in addressing disappointment.

There are the dating books – the majority geared towards women – filled with advice on 'praying for your future husband' and 'becoming God's best while waiting for your man'. There are the ones written by (trying-not-to-sound-smug) married couples, the ones almost exclusively focused on purity and the ones so steeped in gender stereotypes it makes it hard to see the sexism for the trees, and they're all encased in a cover that looks like a family-friendly Mills & Boon illustration. On measure, I think I would feel less self-conscious hiding one of these inside a *Playboy* magazine so I could read it on the bus.

In one book, every anecdote was rounded off with 'and now that person is happily married!', implying that the strength of the illustration was not in the value it added to the individual's spiritual and personal development, but as a stepping stone to wedded bliss. Rather than tackling the problems associated with being single (such as the isolation and feelings of inferiority keenly felt by some single people in the Church), we're desperate to 'solve' relationship statuses with suggestions about online dating or encouragements to pair up with the only other single person vaguely close in age in the congregation.

If you're bored with banal encouragement and well-meaning but ultimately harmful 'problem-solving', you're not alone. I'm bored with talk about dating and 'singleness'. I'm bored with hearing people explore the societal problems that may or may not have led to my relationship status. I'm bored with advice from married people. I'm bored with feeling patronized. I'm bored with gender imbalances and being relegated to children's or women's ministry. It's boring.

Dating is complicated and messy and subjective and individual, and any book that claims a set of rules, way of praying or series of actions will turn things around is fundamentally unhelpful and untrue. What I've found is that, on the whole, people don't feel completely one way about being single. It's rare to find someone who is fully submerged in loneliness and longing, desperately sad and aching to fill the partner-shaped void in their life. Equally it's uncommon to find someone who feels completely satisfied flying solo. Instead, most people go through periods where it's a struggle and periods where it isn't. You don't have to love being single, and I'm not going to tell you to. You don't have to want a husband/wife and I won't tell you to do that either. You're not doing yourself a disservice if you do want to meet someone. You just are where you are, you feel how you feel and, when it comes to dating, there's no amount of manipulating you can (or should) do to speed up the process.

This is not a how-to guide. It's an opportunity to engage, laugh, cry and enjoy the ups and downs of the process. This book is a collection of musings, experiences, absurdity and pain. Think of it as the culmination of all those coffees when you and your mates pore over your profile matches, those heartbroken phone calls to comforting friends and the hilarious mishap tales told over pints at the pub. For me, what started as insightful conversations evolved into recorded interviews. Casual googling turned into research and hours browsing survey data from some of the UK's biggest Christian dating sites. Disjointed ideas and Instagram opinion polls turned into qualitative data. The stories, opinions and ideas in this book have come from a number of sources (all referenced when mentioned): books, articles, peer-reviewed research, surveys, respondents to my social media questions, direct messages, sermons, the Bible, dating courses or one of the focus groups I hosted in order to explore some of these concepts more deeply. I consulted a group of four women, who from here on will be referred to as 'All Saints', and a group of six men I've dubbed 'Foo Fighters' (there weren't many six-piece male groups to choose from).

As this book includes my first-hand experience and a few ghosts of my love life past, it may be helpful to more thoroughly introduce myself. I was brought up as a Christian by a devoted mother, who took me to Sunday school every week. I enjoyed Christ but not Christians and, when I was old enough to be given a choice, I opted out of church. A few years and emotional traumas later and I found myself with a cocaine habit and alcohol problem. It took a number of attempts, a move to Paris and the intervention of friends and family, but on 22 April 2014, I got clean. Five days later I walked back into a church, asked for prayer and I haven't looked back since.

My history of addiction and my resulting sobriety is not a secret – I speak about it a lot, including giving a TEDx Talk on it (2018b). I'm not uncomfortable talking about it; in fact my sobriety is one of the greatest sources of pride in my life. But there is a moment when I meet new people and I have to decide how and when I'm going to slip it into conversation for the first time. I usually awkwardly shoehorn it in as part of my response to a small-talk question. They pull an understanding, yet worldly expression, indicating that they are comfortable with my unfortunate story and that I won't face any of that media-hysteria-induced stigma from them. I make an inappropriate joke. They laugh nervously. They ask a question to further illustrate their ease in handling difficult topics of conversation. I answer and then say I need to go to the bathroom. I never come back.

Aside from it being an interesting story, my recovery is also relevant to this book. I worked the 12-step programme (other methods are available), a process that, with the exception of the first step, is not about drinking or taking drugs but relationships: with yourself, your friends, your family, your partners and God. I've spent the last five years walking hundreds of people through that process through sponsorship/ mentoring and the Recovery Course, which I run from my church. This has provided me with uncommon insight into how people think in relationships and, crucially, how easy it is for them to go wrong and the devastation that can cause. My recovery also means that any dating I have done in church has been completely unlubricated by alcohol – a foreign concept to some, but not as scary as it sounds.

Since cleaning up my act, I trained as a journalist and worked for a few years as a tabloid features writer. During this time, I experimented with dating, trialled apps and techniques and documented the experiences as part of my work. I have recorded myself on a first date at Greggs the Bakers (2018c), standing on the streets of London Bridge trying to literally lasso myself a boyfriend (2018a) and subjected myself to seven dates in seven days from seven niche dating sites (2016). Mouse Mingle for adult Disney lovers led to the most bizarre encounter, although Gluten-Free Singles was a close second. I later wrote a guide on designing an eye-catching profile on Christian swipe-app Salt for the *Church Times* (2019), which people seemed to enjoy (and not just my mate, who was named several times – all publicity is good publicity, eh, Angus?). In addition to this tomfoolery, I have a degree in Neuroscience and a

Master's in Addiction Studies. They are the trump cards I keep hidden for the people who decide I am irreparably ridiculous.

My relationship status has pogoed between 'single', 'in a relation-ship' and 'dating' during the writing and editing of this book. If you get motion sickness you may want to grab a ginger biscuit, because you're coming on that ride with me. While the book is presented in a linear fashion, being single, dating and then true love, this is just because it is simplest – not because it is a representation of life. Ideally, we would all know true love before we get started. Framing the state of things for single people neatly lays the foundations to talk about dating, although you, like me, may delve in and out of the two states. At this very moment, editing the introduction for (what I hope will be) the final time, I am single but bruised after my second break-up of the year. In fact, the note on 'Disappointment' was written just four hours after my first.

I, like the majority, enjoy and endure single life in equal measure. I oscillate between enthusiasm and revulsion when it comes to dating; a swing that is often dictated by the amount of attention I am currently receiving and the temporal proximity of my most recent disappointment. I have talked about my own previous relationships and these passages have been read and approved by the individuals mentioned. Incidentally, every single ex I messaged asked me to change his name to something ridiculous. So where you see a surprising pseudonym, know that some-where out there an ex of mine thinks he's funny. And there was me thinking I didn't have a type.

Although these particular stories are told from my perspective, that of a heterosexual woman, I would be disappointed if that rendered this book inaccessible to anyone outside that group. I've done my best to keep the language gender neutral, but where I can't, please mentally exchange the pronouns if you find it helpful.

While on the topic of words, I have often found the language around being single unhelpful, particularly in the Church. I'm going to do my best to avoid any of this 'other half' or 'the one' ridiculousness. I have even assigned designated 'Christianese-assassins' to proofread and mercilessly eradicate any clichéd Christian terminology; there's no 'doing life' or being 'intentional' here. I'm also not going to use the word 'single' as a noun: a person is not 'a single' or part of a group of 'singles'. Single is not who people are, but one of many aspects that contribute to the richness of their character. It is an adjective.

If these pages fully represented me, they would include a reasonable amount of swearing. I know that's not conventional in a book on faith, but I subscribe to a 'progress not perfection' model. However, as this *is* a Christian book, edited and signed off by the red pens of Christian publishers, I will ditch the obscenities. Instead, when I feel the urge to bash out an expletive on the keyboard, I will simply replace it with '_____'. So you can choose your own word to fill the space. Here are a few my less vulgar friends opt for: flip, fudge, frick, freak, fluff, fiddle-sticks, truck, sugar, shoot, shiver me timbers, crud, crumbs, peeved, heck, darn and dang. Feel free to come up with your own. It's your _____ing choice.

I'm going to struggle to stop feminism creeping in. It's key and rele-vant, but I pledge to you now not to use the words 'patriarchy' or 'vagina'. I'm not here to bash men. I don't hate men at all. On the whole, my male friends are respectable and respectful. They want to date well. They want to leave each person they interact with better than before. That's not to say they're perfect. They do some stupid things. But stupidity isn't gender-specific.

All the research and discussions have led me to one conclusion: being single in the Church needs a rebrand. Unlike the narrative that has infiltrated our impressionable minds, single people aren't left on the shelf, lonely, waiting for a suitor, any suitor, to shimmy over after Holy Communion and say: 'I choose you.' Some are waiting for the right connection, some aren't waiting for anything, some have careers and other dependents to prioritize and some are just enjoying window-shopping and dating.

The term 'marriage-obsessed Church' may get some people's backs up, not least church leaders. I would like to clarify that this is the impression I and the single people I have spoken to have been left with in general. It's Church with a capital 'C' and not a reflection of every, or any individual, church. Yours may get this right; it may be 'mildly marriage-focused' or even just 'marriage-complacent'. Regardless of where your church is on the spectrum, I hope you will find something in these pages helpful, as we all have room for improvement.

While I wholeheartedly believe the Church would benefit from adjusting its attitudes to the single experience, there was a point when I stopped to ask myself if this adjustment required a whole book. Is this using a sledgehammer to crack a nut? Does it even matter that much?

When I was coming to the end of the first draft of this book, I had a coffee with my friend Ali. Ali's passion is in creating stunning settings in which people can connect; she doesn't lay a table, she *crafts* it. She hosts intimate dinners where single Christians can meet (and potentially date), describing the initiative as 'connecting Christians living parallel lives'. These events started in New York but migrated with Ali across the pond in 2020. As we chatted, she told me that on the day of the first event, she was under huge spiritual attack. Everything went wrong, she got lost, she felt stressed and panicked and the carefully laid plans went to pot. I am well aware of the dangers of spiritual attack in front-line ministry. Running the recovery programmes for addicts, I've heard stories of people being on their way to share their sobriety testimony when they bump into their old dealer on the street and relapse. Some of those stories end in death. I've experienced the ferocity of self-doubt and emotional ambush myself. But my first thought when Ali was talking was: why would this be under attack?

It's not that important. It's not life or death. It's just *dating*.

That was wrong. This is important. And it's important to God. This book isn't going to be a theological deep-dive but it is written by someone whose life is in service to him and guided by the eternal truth veining through the Bible. And, though there is no modern dating within its pages, the Bible has a lot to say about love, relationships, passion and life. This stuff is important. It was important to the case study in Sonya Sharma's book, *Women and Religion in the West: Challenging secularization* (2008), who felt so marginalized in her church that she left – not just the church but her faith entirely. It was important to the bloke who responded to Single Friendly Church's 2012 survey with: 'I found going to church one of the loneliest places in the world. That is why I no longer attend.' Or the respondent who said: 'To be honest . . . my faith is weaker than ever, as I am angry with God for the situation that I am in.'

So what's the solution? And not to the 'problem' of being single. Is it in changing our attitudes towards single people? Is it in addressing our incessant idolization of marriage? Is it in challenging the way we choose to communicate with people who are struggling? Is it by creating more opportunities for people to find partners? Is it in revolutionizing how we live in community so a person can be single but never lonely?

Yes, but more on all that to come.

Part 1
SINGLE FILE

Things we shouldn't say to single people (and some suggested responses)

Why aren't you married? You're attractive, funny and clever.
Yeh, I'm actually overqualified.

I know you're single, but here's a plus one to my wedding anyway.
Great, I'll bring Sydney from accounting, who will be in your wedding photos (but not my life) for all eternity.

We're all sharing with our other halves for this weekend. Who are you sharing with?
Me? I'll be paying the single-occupancy rate and face-planting the mini bar.

So when's it your turn to settle down and get married?
I'm not sure. I did take a ticket when I came in, but I think I may have missed them calling my number when I nipped to the loo.

Just use this time to work on yourself.
I can't wait till I'm married when I don't need to do any personal development of any kind.

You'll find someone.
This is life, John. Not a giant game of hide-and-seek.

Jesus is your lover.
Thanks, well-meaning person I don't know that well in church. While Jesus is great, there are still some specifically human desires I'm hoping to satisfy this side of glory.

Are you getting yourself out there?
If I can get the coordinates for 'out there', I'll head over right now.

Awww, I'm sorry to hear you're single.
Could you pop that into a get-well-soon card with a 'cheer-me-up' fiver?

If you're still single by 30 you should freeze your eggs.
Cheers, Mum. Would a puppy satiate your desire for grandchildren?

Singled out in the Church

At some point, the Christian perspective on being married and being single seems to have become skewed. Sometimes it can feel like we've subconsciously assigned meaning to each state, ranking them from best to worst and proceeding to make assumptions about individuals in those categories. They can go a bit like this . . .

Married people are the successful, most desirable ones. Single people are the less attractive pool, who will hopefully learn to settle for each other in order that everyone gets paired off. Deliberately single people are deeply suspicious and could surface in years to come as part of a sex scandal uncovered by an investigative journalist. No one's said this from a pulpit; it's not in your church newsletter. It's just ingrained, dripping from every sceptical look and sympathetic glance. But where have these, albeit hyperbolized, assumptions come from?

Married versus single: finding the superior path

Marriage is good. There is implicit beauty in committing to combine your life with another person – prioritizing someone over everyone else (including yourself), loving, caring for, supporting and encouraging that person. God says it is not good for anyone to be alone (Genesis 2.18). God blesses marriage (Matthew 19.6). God encourages people to go forth and multiply (Genesis 1.28).

Aware of the strength of the argument for marriage but unable to testify to its perks myself, I called on two friends, Sophia and James, who married two years ago, to fill in the gaps. They are a couple I believe do marriage well. They haven't cut out friendships in order to hibernate together; they serve at church but on different teams; they celebrate each other's independence. I asked them what was so great about marriage.

SOPHIA: There is a safety in the covenant of marriage, in knowing that that person is not going to leave you. In marriage, I've shown parts of myself that I was scared to show anyone before. It is challenging but I have more confidence in my abilities now. James is constantly pushing me to believe more of myself.

JAMES: I've found the depth to which you are seen and known and you know the other person to be an incredibly vulnerable and fulfilling experience. It's different from the one I've had living with friends.

Not all marriages reflect Sophia and James's experience and they acknowledge that. They also freely acknowledge that they don't always get it right. Regardless, the relationship between husband and wife is used as imagery in the Bible for the relationship between Jesus and those who follow him. Christ is the groom and the Church is the bride (Ephesians 5.25–27). In the same way that a bride and groom are traditionally kept apart in the run-up to their union, the parallel is that, in this current time, Christ is separate from those who believe in him, and their job is to remain faithful to him. The idea is that, when Jesus comes again, this will be the perfect union, the wedding between bride and groom (Revelation 19.7–9; 21.1–20).

With the model of a wedding being used to illustrate the relationship between Christ and the Church, it's easy to see why Christians revere the institution of marriage. But there are a number of indications in the Bible that marriage is not the pinnacle of lived existence. Start by looking at the single people: author-of-28-per-cent-of-the-New-Testament Paul, prophet-and-forerunner-in-Eastern-Christianity John the Baptist and Son-of-God Jesus. These aren't supporting characters. They aren't in the chorus line. Without them we wouldn't have the New Testament or indeed Christianity. Both Paul and John were human and flawed, so feasibly could have got the decision not to marry wrong. But Jesus lived a sin-free, exemplary life. His remaining single was not based on poor judgement. If the headliners of Christianity didn't think it important to 'take a wife' in order to live life to the full, why should we?

In my research, I've heard marriage described as a 'whole-making' covenant between two people. I've read books that suggest that, as a man and woman are made in God's image, we can only represent him in his fullness in marriage. But I don't think that's what God's saying. The Bible is clear when it explicitly states that, through Christ, we are complete – no exchanging of vows required (Colossians 2.9–10).

Back in the day (way back in the Old Testament days), the most prized achievement for the Jews was continuing the family line. God's ultimate blessing to his people was promising them an abundance of descendants (Genesis 12.2; 22.17; 26.4). Jon Tyson, a preacher at Church of the City New York, in his talk 'Singleness' (2018) explains that, for the Romans, dignity came from your ability to procreate: a woman's value was in the children she produced, particularly the male children. But then scriptures came along and said: 'There is no longer Jew or Greek, there is no longer slave or free, there is no longer male and female; for all of you are one in Christ Jesus' (Galatians 3.28, NRSV). Jon explained: 'One theologian said: "This is the most radical reorientation of the value of personhood in recorded history." What Jesus was saying is that your value and your dignity weren't tied to your social standing in the Roman family.' He gave dignity back to the individual. In the resurrection, with Jesus' promise of eternal life, there is no need to marry and procreate so as to secure a life that outlasts our physical bodies.

A second blow for marriage as an ideal is Jesus' revelation that in heaven no one will be married (Mark 12.25). Death hits 'reset' on all your relationships. We're all equal individuals, part of God's big family. No knots tied, no getting hitched, Gretna Green officially out of business. If heaven is the place God has designed for us (Hebrews 11.10, 16), a paradise (Luke 23.43) where all our needs are met (Revelation 7.16–17) and marriage isn't there, God can't think we actually need it.

The biggest advocate of single life was, of course, Paul. In his letters to the Corinthians the apostle encouraged people to stay unmarried as he was (1 Corinthians 7.8). He described the split interests of a married person compared to someone single who can fully focus on God (1 Corinthians 7.32–35), a practice modelled by Jesus himself. Cut back to Jon Tyson: 'Jesus, who is the archetype of all true humanity, was single. Fully man, suffering as we do, relying on the power of the Holy Spirit, Jesus was single. He used his singleness to serve. This is a major affirmation for single people.'

The fact is, neither is better. When a person gets married, or indeed becomes 'un-married', they are not trading one inferior state for a superior one or vice versa. It's just a transition from one setting to another. Being single is something everyone will experience and if they have the desire to get married and circumstances allow, they can. But this is not a levelling-up process. They are trading the perks and challenges of flying solo with the perks and challenges of pairing off. Fullness, oneness, wholeness are present and available in both these states through Jesus.

Gift of singleness

What about this 'gift of singleness' that people bandy around? Could this be the present everyone secretly hopes God kept the receipt for? The overwhelming impression I've got through my research for this book is that many of us are harbouring secret fears our name is on that gift list and are desperately praying that God alleviates us from the blessing. If God was the sorting hat, being single would be Slytherin and we'd be petitioning like Potter for access to Gryffindor.

Al Hsu, author of *The Single Issue* (1998), explains his view that the concept is unhelpful. He makes the point that both marriage and singleness are a gift and you have whichever one relates to your present state. That state, and therefore that gift, can change. A problem he highlights is that by discussing it as a 'gift', you're suggesting that being single is something that can only be endured and enjoyed through this anointing. In Sam Allberry's book, *7 Myths About Singleness* (2019), he explains that considering it a gift implies that being single is second best and requires divine levels of endurance. Where would that leave you if you were currently single but didn't believe you had been given 'the gift'? Would you just have to white-knuckle until you could find a lifeboat (husband/wife) to cling on to?

All this pigeonholing and selective anointing just doesn't sit with our understanding of the grace-filled, loving God. When I think about God's character, it feels more likely that he allows us the dignity of choice when it comes to our relationships. This was affirmed when I spoke to Sophia and James about the start of their relationship.

JAMES: I felt passionate about the idea of living a single life and being fully available to serve God in whatever way I was called to within that. But then I met Sophia and I asked God what I was supposed to do. I really felt God gave me the choice. What I heard was: "If you choose Sophia, I'm going to honour that, with the good and bad consequences, whatever they may be. But if you choose to stay single, I'm going to honour that, with the good and bad consequences, whatever they may be."

I truly believe that God wants our options to be open and for us to choose to pursue the set-up that allows us to connect most deeply with him; not to trap and push us into something that doesn't feel right or sit comfortably.

For a number of reasons, there are people who take the decision not to date and there is nothing wrong with this. In fact, it comes with a lot of perks. There are also a number of people who have taken the decision to commit to being single because they are resigned to the idea that they won't find a partner. They'd rather save themselves the bother and heartache and stay single, feeling more comfortable knowing that they've taken matters into their own hands and have control of their relationship status.

The Church: a roast

I've called this section 'a roast' because what follows isn't pretty. I'm about to outline the modern Church's position – or at least people's perception of its position – on being single. Don't think of this as a take-down. Think of me as the loving but fed-up parent, who's come home from a tense parent–teacher conference and is reporting to the other parent what their little _____ – sorry, angel – has been doing at school. This is from a place of love, but also frustration and the hope of development.

Note that a church is not just a building; it's also not just its leadership (although leaders naturally have significant influence). It is the congregation, the body of people who gather there and call it home. In other words, this is relevant for you. Each individual member of the Church is responsible for forming its attitudes and responses.

Conversation

First up, as you've seen from the first note, there are some unhelpful ways of speaking to single people and this is classic in church congregations. One of the people I interviewed pointed out: 'People who say, "God provides" or "God will make it happen", don't realize that that just makes me wonder if I'm not good enough for God to make it happen for me.' Another interviewee, who is single in their fifties, had even had someone in church suggest they were cursed. In Sonya Sharma's book, _Women and Religion in the West: Challenging secularization_ (2008), the author immersed herself in a British Newfrontiers church. During that time, she observed that four out of five of the conversations about being single were negative, casting it as a state of waiting for a partner. She offered 'you'd better hurry up' and 'you shouldn't be so fussy' as examples typical of the conversations.

Preaching

If the coffee and chat at the back of church would be awarded a C–, then the preaching from the front isn't even scraping a passing grade. James, who seriously considered committing to single life, pointed out: 'I didn't experience any discussion around being single as a good thing from church leaders. There wasn't talk about the advantages of being single even just for a short-term period.'

The 'woefully inadequate' (quote from Bella) teaching on the topic was also flagged up in a huge survey of 3,000 single Christians, 'Singleness in the UK Church', conducted by Single Friendly Church (set up by the team behind dating site Christian Connection) in 2012. One participant said: 'The pain of singleness is never acknowledged or prayed about because it is preached as a gift. I therefore find the pain very isolating.'

On taking the issue to my focus groups, the feeling was similar. All Saints (the four women) recalled an annual talk on relationships that would often major on sex as being the only vaguely relevant church teaching, while Foo Fighters (the six blokes) felt that even within normal preaching, the examples and anecdotes often excluded single people. One said: 'We don't need to hear constant illustrations using your kids in the sermon.'

Focus on marriage

The undeniable fact is that the Church as a whole has an emphasis on marriage. Researcher David Voas conducted a quantitative analysis of Church life with a survey and found the majority of English church attendees are married. He said: 'It's hardly an exaggeration to say that in England individuals don't go to church, couples do.'

People who run churches are usually married men and their partners take up a first-lady position in doting support. Single Friendly Church's survey (2012) found 43 per cent of single people felt their church didn't know what to do with them. Ministry for single people, if it exists, is often an afterthought and not engineered in a way that makes it appealing to potential attendees. Two thirds of people in the Single Friendly Church's survey said they felt being married is the expected and accepted lifestyle in the Church. So much so that the Church is based around the school calendar with everything effectively shutting down over August.

I've heard of people trying to set up initiatives for single people but being told by church leaders that, as they themselves were single, they probably weren't best placed. I've heard of 'pairs and spares' dinners and people being relegated to 'all-singles groups' (the equivalent of the kids' table at Christmas).

Someone, somewhere came up with the genius idea of having speakers at a festival walk on stage with their partners, who introduce themselves before scuttling off to leave the preachers to it. But, if they're not specifically talking about marriage, what's the point? Would an advertising exec start a pitch by handing round pictures of his wife and two adorable children? Perhaps waiters should adjust their intro spiel to: 'Hi, I'm Nathan. I'll be your waiter this evening. My wife is named Rosie and we've been together for six years now. Can I take your order?' I was once at a conference with two male speakers and one female. Both men had their wives make meek introductions before they delivered their talks, while the (also married) woman walked out alone. In fact, I have seen this bizarre phenomenon countless times, but not once have I seen a husband walk on stage as a hype man for his wife. I've heard Australian evangelist Christine Cain joke about it, though.

One of the All Saints flagged up a similar observation: 'Every time there's an announcement that someone is being sent off to plant a new church, it's always a married couple. I just want to see one of those announcements for someone single for once.'

Volunteering and leadership

To add insult to injury, there are churches that won't allow unmarried people into positions of leadership. One study found that half the American churches quizzed wouldn't allow a single person to run a house group. 'A new bloke wants to run a Bible study? We'll need to see a marriage certificate from this Jesus chap if he wants to head up small groups in this church.'

One respondent to the Single Friendly Church's survey (2012) said: 'One of the things that eventually led to me drifting away from committed attendance was when, at a church meeting, one member stood up and said, on the subject of appointing a youth minister, that "only a married person would be acceptable, as that was the right role model of relationships for their children". I don't think this person can possibly have realized how insulting that was to those who were struggling to remain hopeful despite the isolation of singleness.'

This should be obvious; someone getting married does not suddenly qualify that person for leadership. It's an incredibly damaging and short-sighted view. Single people are often the most time-rich and therefore, in terms of ministry, a church's biggest asset. They aren't bound by nap times and routine. They aren't juggling a social life made up of two sets of friends and family. Yes, they are often busy, but with things they choose to do and far fewer non-negotiable obligations. During 2020's COVID-19 lockdown, I coordinated a team of church volunteers who could support vulnerable people in our parish with shopping, errands and prescription collections. When I looked at my list of volunteers, I always jumped for the single people first. In the fast-paced, uncertain times, I needed people who could just mobilize, and experience showed me that they were best placed to do that. Married people and those with families were incredibly valuable, but far more likely to respond the following day or send a placeholder while they checked with their partner what they would be able to commit to. There is nothing wrong with that at all. But at a time of relative emergency, it was the single people who carried the operation.

There are also examples of churches swinging too far the other way and expecting single people to carry the full burden of the church's workload. A few respondents to the survey said they felt 'like useful labour', 'exploited for service' or 'treated like a household servant for a family'. One of All Saints told me about a friend who, as the only single person at her church, took on Sunday school every single week without fail, to allow the married couples a childcare break.

Socializing

Another source of upset is the way people socialize and welcome others in churches. In the Single Friendly Church survey (2012), respondents felt the Church didn't recognize the need for a social network for single people. One said: 'One couple asked me to dinner once they realized I had a boyfriend. How much more I needed that invite before I had the boyfriend.' Another interviewee expressed sadness at the regular games nights hosted by church friends, which they were never invited to because they didn't have a partner.

Celebrations

The constant celebrating of others' milestones was a source of discomfort for some. One of the All Saints said: 'Being single is not put down but it's just not subject to the same celebration. The lack of festivities for single people perpetuates the idea that being in a couple equates to success and being single doesn't. We need to make more of a fuss of people moving out on their own or getting a new job.' A survey respondent said: 'We celebrate Mother's/Father's Day, family services, youth events. We clap for weddings/anniversaries. If you're single, you just watch – those are not the biggest achievements of life.' As Carrie Bradshaw (*Sex and the City*) puts it: 'If you are single after graduation, there isn't one occasion where people celebrate you. Hallmark doesn't make a "congratulations you didn't marry the wrong person" card. Where's the flatware for going on vacation alone?'

Where does this leave single people?

With marriage presented as the normative status in the Church, Sonya Sharma (2008) points out that there will always be an expectation that that behaviour will occur. This leaves us with a group who are trying to work out how they fit into the church family.

There are swathes of people who are terrified they are becoming less desirable in the marketplace every time more Christians blow out the candles on their twenty-first birthday cakes; who are unsure if they should settle for something less than love to appease loneliness and claim their place among the couples; who are disillusioned with church; who are panicking that there aren't enough eligible Christian people left to date; who are unsure of the appropriate levels of vulnerability in dating but deeply in need of connection; who are questioning if they are being punished by God; who are convinced they were supposed to be rewarded for their righteousness and don't understand where God is any more.

One person I interviewed welled up, saying: 'I had got to a point where I was OK, but I'm not there any more. It's not about me and other people. It's about me and God. If he can do anything – if he can move mountains – then why doesn't he do it for me? If I'm meant to be single, I wish he'd let me know. Then I can stop searching.'

This group of people are crying out for church leaders to stop patronizing them and offering them unhelpful answers, and, instead, to acknowledge that, if they were in their shoes, they would find it hard too. There is room to address this pain and fear in preaching but, at the moment, few are stepping up to fill the void. I care a lot about these issues and a lot of single people I know do too. But each of us who relates to these sentiments needs to ask, 'Would I be so keen to shift the culture and debate the problems if I suddenly got engaged? Am I investing more of my energy into fixing the injustice or into getting married, so I can stop paying my dues and be on the beneficial side of the inequality?'

Running out of time

The right time

As part of my research for this project, I came across a section in someone else's book where they addressed the big question: 'What is the right age to get married?' I know what you're thinking and I agree: life is too nuanced, too diverse, too unique to specify a timeline for anything. That's the beauty of the rich tapestry that forms our individual journeys and the joy and trials of life's surprising twists and turns. Nope. She went for 25.

According to this expert, 25 is the right age for wedlock. Any younger and you don't know your mind; any older and you're set in your ways. In marriage terms, 25 is the baby bear's porridge; not too hot, not too cold – it's just right. It's the first time I'd heard someone so firmly plant their flag on this topic, but I have previously been aware of an insidious attitude, not openly acknowledged but felt by many, that people should be married before 30.

I took this to my interviewees. One 30-year-old bloke's response was: 'Does that mean you've missed the boat if you're not Christian when you're 25? This kind of thinking isn't grounded in the real world. It'll just lead to disappointment for everyone when it doesn't work out.' Another interviewee, Grace, a woman in her fifties, told me about Uncle Milton's wedding. I vaguely remember Uncle Milton from church growing up, but what I didn't know as a child is that Uncle Milton had been married twice and both his wives had devastatingly passed away from cancer. After the death of his second wife, he was single and in his seventies.

Grace said: 'This man never gave up on hope that he would meet someone else. In the end, he was remarried at 76. It was the most beautiful wedding I've ever been to. There was something in the atmosphere – it was God's love and their love. They were so happy. It just proved to me that you can be any age and get married. There's always hope.'

Let me take this opportunity to dispel the falsehood: there is no correct timeline for anything. If we're using the Bible as an example of how God works in people's lives, we can all acknowledge that God introduces things 'out of sync' with the norm. People have children far later than modern medicine would deem it possible. People start their ministry young or achieve incredible things in old age. There is no formula or one size fits all or age-based milestone that has to be hit. God is not formulaic.

One of All Saints added: 'This perceived timeline makes people feel pressured to make bad decisions and makes us feel like failures.' Allowing ourselves to believe that we should be adhering to a schedule leads to one of two things: pushing yourself to conform to a cookie-cutter existence, squeezing yourself to what you think are the world's ideals when that may be far from what God has for you. Or otherwise, if you think you're not keeping up with these checkpoints, you feel inadequate. This leads to stress and pressure.

Comparing your situation to the situations of those around you is damaging. It's not fruitful and life-giving. It's not God. The fact is, the right time for any milestone is when you – in collaboration with God – say it is. It's unlikely to be the same as what is the right time for those around you. And you don't need to restrict yourself with deadlines. You haven't failed if you don't get married at 25.

Acknowledging what you want

There was a girl in my class at school, who rocked up at the sports hall for exams and would announce loudly to anyone who would listen that she hadn't done any revision and she was definitely _____ed. She completed this ritual like clockwork before every test and then went on to get top grades.

Why is it such a problem to acknowledge what you want and be seen to be taking active steps towards achieving that goal? What's the worst that would happen if she said: 'I've worked really hard. I'll be upset if I do badly.' You don't need to play it cool before your GCSEs and you *don't* need to play it cool with dating. You can act nonchalant all you want but if you're sitting the exam, you want to pass and if you're going on a date, you want it to go well.

Is time ticking away?

There is only one thing, when it comes to relationships, that has a time stamp and there's no point pretending it's not there. If you want to have biological children, you won't be able to do that for ever. There is an age when women can't have children; there's also an age when men shouldn't. Just because you've got yeast in the pot at the age of 80 doesn't mean you should bake bread.

Having biological children is not the only way to experience parenting and to be part of a family. If you want to support and bring up children, there are plenty whose parents don't have the ability or inclination to fully take on that role. We can foster or adopt, or just be present and consistent for a child in our community/church/family/street, who otherwise would lack positive adult attention. When God said to go forth and multiply, there wasn't a surplus of people who already needed our care on a run-down, over-populated earth.

Here I refer to a great friend of mine. Clare is an exceptional person, who moved out of London a few years ago in order to foster. When quizzed on the topic, she said: 'In society, and especially in church circles, we seem to believe it is our right to have children rather than a privilege. We are not owed children. That's where we've got to change. As soon as we start seeing children as a privilege, regardless of whether they are biological, adopted, fostered or your best friend's kids, it changes our understanding of family. The kingdom of God is about an invitation extended to all. This includes the stranger. So, whether it's a child we've found and pinpointed and chosen or a child we've made, it's all family. Adoption points us to God because we've all experienced adoption into his family.'

Children are wonderful; you're obviously not a terrible person for having them or wanting them. It's just important you don't feel trapped by that desire. If you don't procreate, it doesn't mean you've failed at life. It is not the meaning of life. There are plenty of people whose lives you can help restore, who you can help make new, without contributing to their DNA. Ultimately the idea that you're running out of time is a lie. It is something to be challenged every time it comes into your head. God is bigger than time. God doesn't run out of time. It is a lie that we allow to take hold because it is rooted in a deep fear. 'Do not be afraid' is the most common instruction in the Bible. Decisions made from fear are bad decisions. Fear is not stable ground on which to build a life; it needs to be challenged and eradicated every time it crops up. Don't let those thoughts sink in. Take them captive and make them obedient to Christ (2 Corinthians 10.5). Base your decisions on what is good: justice, conviction, hope, love, peace and a true understanding of your value in Jesus. When you get those things in place, that's when we're cooking on gas.

Should I pray?

Is it mad to pray for a partner? Isn't that a bit cringey? No. Definitely pray that you will meet someone you can team up with, who shares your passion and vision and ultimately will add value to your spiritual and physical life. But don't let that be your only prayer. Don't become all-consumed by that prayer and unable to move on from that topic until you're satisfied it's been answered. What if God decided you were the only person in the world whose prayer requests he would listen to? Just you; no one else. What would you pray for then? If you knew that, would you spend every night on your knees asking for a husband/wife? We've got bigger fish to fry, people. Pray for your family, pray for each of your friends, your leaders, your community, your church, the world, persecution, modern slavery, abuse and domestic violence. While you're focusing on petitioning for a partner, a world of praise, gratitude and intercession is passing you by. Let God know what you want, for sure, but be part of the bigger effort and allow it to take its rightful place.

Missing out

If you continue to count others' milestones and focus on what you don't have, you're going to miss something amazing. Let me tell you Norris's firework story. She (yep, 'she', her real name's Naomi – I wish I could explain, but I honestly don't know) was lying in bed praying. She'd just taken a hit with her love life and was feeling low. In front of her was a wall-mounted print of the London skyline. As she watched it, she got a picture of the huge New Year's Eve fireworks display that happens every year on the river. Over to one side, she spotted a couple messing around with sparklers. They were laughing and flirting and generally having a jovial time. She wanted what they had. But then in this picture, God told her to stop watching them and to look up. Right in front of her was a beautiful firework display. Not just a couple of bangers; we're talking the ones that corkscrew up and then glitter into a thousand cascading lights and those massive weeping-willow ones. There was probably also a Catherine wheel, although admittedly Norris never mentioned it. Moral of the story: watch the fireworks not the sparklers. What if God's putting on a stunning show right in front of you, but you're missing it because you're too busy watching people make a hash of spelling out their names with a flaming stick?

I'm not immune to these thoughts of comparison. A while back, I expressed my disappointment at not hitting some professional and personal milestones to my therapist. I told her that the worry about my achievements was taking up a huge amount of my headspace. I ended my explanation with: 'So I guess that's wrong.' To which she replied: 'Lauren, I don't know if it's *wrong*. But is it worth it?'

Is it worth it? Is worrying ever worth it? One of my most formative experiences as a Christian was when I first sat down to read the Bible, aged 25. My mum insisted that Genesis was not the right place to start so set me off with Matthew. It was when I got to Jesus' words from the Sermon on the Mount: 'Can any one of you by worrying add a single hour to your life?' (Matthew 6.27, NIV) that I realized there was something special here. That's the moment I realized the Bible wasn't all full of zoo-boats and miracle-strengthening hair. That's when I realized that this Jesus had some things to say that were worth listening to. Yet here I am, years on, still having to remind myself of the fundamental truth: worrying achieves nothing.

Do you reinforce the idea that you're running out of time by comparing yourself to other people? Let me ask you this – when reading this book, have you tried to work out how old I am? Have you wondered if I'm good-looking or overweight? Would it reassure you to be able to explain away my relationship status, because 'I'm not as attractive as you' so you're still in with a chance? If you see that I'm four years older than you, does that act as reassurance that 'you've still got time'? Equally, if I turn out to be four years younger than you, is that depressing? Does it render my experience of being single invalid because it hasn't lasted as long as yours? What if I start seeing someone or get engaged? Would that be disheartening and amount to a loss of credibility? The fact is that none of these factors actually matters, particularly if you find something here you relate to. Every time I see a new reality TV star is pregnant, the first thing I do is google their age, as if that person being older than I am buys me time, while being younger serves to pile on more pressure. We all just need to stop.

Stop watching the clock

The fact is, you may or may not be single for ever; that is partly your choice and partly circumstances beyond your control. No one can promise you anything. But I can promise you, 80-year-old-you won't thank you for wasting years pining after something you don't have, whether you eventually get it or not. Life is for the living. If you don't fully invest in it, you will miss something. You'll miss the freedom, the uninterrupted friend time, the financial flexibility, the space, the autonomy. These are all gifts.

Regardless of the relationship status you want, on this day you have the one you have and it's your job to live it to the fullest: to make the most of it, connected to God and in service of others. It is possible to find peace and contentment in single life and still hope to meet someone. Just as it is possible to live single life well while still preferring not to be single.

Don't treat being single like temporary accommodation. It's not the flat you're renting before you have a kid and get a bigger place out of town. This is your current circumstance and even if it lasts only another two months, it's still worth fully investing in. Buy furniture, put the pictures up on the wall, unpack and make yourself at home. Don't be superstitious and think if you get comfy, God will get confused and think you never wanted to meet someone. Live in the moment you are in and embrace those circumstances. Don't allow yourself to dwell on what has or hasn't happened or fret about what's to come. They say: 'Addicts have one foot in the past, one foot in the future and are pissing on the present.' I think all of us can slip into that from time to time. There's something special right in front of us, if we stop comparing, stop counting, stop telling ourselves where we 'should' be. Don't wish you had someone else's sparkler when God's putting on a firework display in your honour.

Being single: pros and cons

✔ Your home habits are yours and yours alone – you have no one to answer to for leaving toenail clippings on the bedside table or eating cereal straight out of the box.

✘ You can't always reach the bit between your shoulders when putting on sun cream. And if that patch gets burnt, you can't reach it with the after-sun either.

✔ You're not related to anyone other than your own actual family. No in-laws, no politics, no uncomfortable Christmases round theirs; no juggling of relations you're doing your very best to love as if they were yours.

✘ The feeling you may be letting people down and not meeting their expectations by not finding a partner.

✔ You can decorate your room/house to your taste. You can put up your own photos of people you like and faces you want to see. There's no one to insist on more soft furnishings or telling you to take down your 'Live, laugh, love' sign because it's too 'basic'.

✘ Missing out on the additional prayer power of having someone else petitioning God for the things you care about too. Plus the comfort of actually sitting down to pray with someone who knows you deeply.

✔ Your friends can be your priority. You can go out-out, have movie/videogame/sport marathons and go for dinners and coffees without being accused of neglecting your partner.

✘ Those moments when you realize you're the only single person at an event and have to overcompensate by explaining how cool you are with it.

✔ There's no guilt in spending time on your own, or just not wanting to call someone that night or turning your phone off. There's no one to offend with introversion.

31

✘ Not having the regular physical contact with someone who deeply respects and cares about you. Not having that person there to kiss, touch, have sex with.

✔ You can spend your money however you like. If you want to drop £200 on an old action-hero toy (pristine condition in box) that you wanted as a child but your mum never bought you (you know who you are), then you don't need to ask anyone.

✘ Not having the perks of a dual income – splitting of rent and bills means more financial stability. Plus it's two people's responsibility to dredge through the financial life-admin.

✔ You can make and change plans on a whim, without syncing diaries or checking if they're OK with it or organizing childcare. You are untethered. Unfastened. Free to blow in the wind as you please.

✘ You can feel lonely not having someone to come home to. While your friends are great, there's a depth of companionship and consistency from a relationship that it's hard to replicate.

✔ Beds are comfier when you spread out on your own *adopts starfish position*.

✘ It's more feasible to be able to get a dog when two people can take charge of the pup-keep.

✔ You get to date, which can mean fun activities, food you've never tried, pushing yourself out of your comfort zone, meeting new people and accumulating some hilarious stories.

✘ You get to date, which means you're suddenly at the mercy of a stranger, and the level to which they find you interesting can have a real effect on you.

✔ You don't need to worry about body maintenance as it's only you who's seeing it. Shave, don't shave, tan, don't tan, swap abs day for pie and mash? The choice is yours.

✘ The feeling of everyone around you pairing off is akin to realizing you're the last person still in a temporary birthday WhatsApp group. They just left you behind.

Being single: pros and cons

✔ You can choose where to travel to, enjoy solo holidays and take yourself off on an 'eat, pray, love' if you want. You don't need to navigate two people's annual leave and commitments. It's just you, your passport and the open road. A bit like Jack Kerouac but hopefully less misogynistic and resulting in a less boring memoir (don't @ me).

✘ If you cook yourself dinner, you also have to do the washing-up. That includes washing, drying and putting away. And, by the time you've paid the delivery fee, a takeaway for one person is a real extravagance.

✔ Without the responsibility of another person or a family, you can commit to helping others and serving God in a way you just couldn't in a relationship.

✘ People assuming that, as you're single, you've got free time to do their bidding.

✔ You can pee with the door open and leave the seat in whichever position you prefer (not recommended if you have flatmates).

✘ If there's a leak, or the fire alarm goes off, or a flatpack needs assembling, or your engine is making a knocking sound, or you have to fix the toilet, or cancel a bank card, all that labour and/or admin is on you alone.

✔ Your Netflix recommendations reflect your actual preferences and not a weird amalgamation of the two of you. How are they supposed to make helpful suggestions when you're viewing *Pitch Perfect* and the *Greatest Events of WWII in Colour* on the same weekend?

✘ Turning up to a wedding on your own means perfecting the circuit between the bar, toilet and dancefloor so that you don't get caught alone in one place for too long. It also means single-occupancy room rates, no group travel discounts, no splitting of cab fares and no one to keep you company when the bride is an hour late and you're starving hungry in a freezing-cold church.

✔ You get to flirt with whoever you like, guilt-free.
✘ Fancying someone and realizing they're married.

✔ You don't have to compromise on what music/podcasts/audio books you listen to or films you watch. You can put Eiffel 65 on repeat if that's your thing.

✘ You can't tell knock-knock jokes to yourself. You can't challenge yourself to a game of chess or Kerplunk. You can't ride a tandem or a seesaw. You can't high five yourself. You can't play table tennis on your own – apart from when people prop up one side of the table and play against it like it's a wall. That's actually pretty cool.

Are you ready to date?

The chapter 'Are you ready to date?' comes up in one form or another in virtually every Christian dating book I've read. How to prepare yourself to date; how to lay the groundwork now for a strong future relationship; how to 'become a person that the person you want to date, wants to date'. I'll save you the trouble of rifling through another ten books and give you the executive summary here.

- This time of being single can still be positive for your dating life, because it gives you the space to grow into a better future partner (in other words, the best time to work on your relationship is before you're in it).
- Recommended areas of growth include (but are not limited to): ensuring your finances are in order, addressing any debt; general character development; not chasing cheap thrills and quick fixes; looking after yourself and managing your house well; being motivated, getting a job and starting your career; identifying addictions; addressing anything holding you back from spiritual, emotional and relational health; committing to a local church.
- It may be helpful to take a period out where you deliberately don't date – a 'season of singleness' – to reflect on yourself.

You're likely to have heard this before. It's a familiar rhetoric. The problem with the first two bullet points is that they are great *life* advice. Personal development is not only relevant to those who hope to be in a romantic relationship. Equally, to expect that married people have already done this or don't need to is ridiculous. By listing these things in a book for single people you're saying: work harder and you'll find love. And that is _____.

One book I read suggested asking yourself how your future partner would view your spending habits as part of the process of self-development. Are they serious? To be clear, this book was asking you to imagine what a theoretical human being would think of your finances and then adjust your habits to what is assumed will be more palatable to that *pretend* person. This has got to be a joke. What about what *you* think of your spending? And more importantly than that, what does *God* think of your spending? Have you asked him? Have you read some of Jesus' teachings on money (of which there are a lot)? Are you confident that your charitable giving and tithing are in line with his heart? Are you confident that you're giving away enough that money doesn't have any power over you? That you are submitting your money to God's will and trusting him with your security? If you're not sure about this, get stuck in: buy Richard Foster's book, *Money, Sex and Power* (1985). Google Jesus' parables on money and some commentaries. Pray about it. But whatever you do, don't make it your mission to adapt yourself to a person you haven't even met yet.

On the topic of money, I think it's key to flag up, you don't need to be rich to date. You don't need to financially cripple yourself taking people out. If you just don't have the budget for dinners, keep it low-key and take a couple of sandwiches to the park. But don't hold off for pay cheques or promotions. The person will be interested in your company not your bank balance, and if they're not, you've had a touch working that out so early.

Another source of frustration is that the idea of managing your household well is often directed towards women, sometimes subtly and sometimes not, and the idea of settling into a good career is often angled towards men. I wish it were redundant to say these are applicable both ways. No one, regardless of gender, should be an adult who doesn't know how to use a washing machine or a laundrette. No one should be confused about how to pay the bills at home or where the fuse board is or how to call out an emergency plumber. Because it makes you a better partner? No. Because it makes you a functioning adult. Equally, everyone, again gender not relevant, should explore the idea of establishing themselves in a job they are excited by. It doesn't have to be highly paid; it doesn't have to be full time. For some, it will be a job caring for someone in their life; for others it will be pounding the corridors of an intimidatingly large glass building in the City. Is this because you're going to need to be a breadwinner for your future wife, two angelic children and dog called Flopsie? No. It's because you can find purpose, challenges, opportunities to work well and demonstrate God's kingdom in your job, as well as establishing financial security for yourself.

General character development, identifying addictions and working through anything that's holding you back from spiritual, emotional and relational health are, at the heart of it, all along the same lines. They are really important. I'm not against personal development at all. I think literally everyone would benefit from working the 12 steps of recovery (a formula designed by the early attendees of Alcoholics Anonymous meetings to help each other establish and maintain sobriety. See my TEDx Talk (2018b) for more info – I'm aware that I just plugged myself, which is a _____ move, but I do think I cover the main points in that presentation and I'm not doing it again here).

I just don't think personal development should be in order to better yourself for your future partner. You're already adapting to being who someone else wants you to be and you haven't even met that person yet. Why not work out who you are? Clean house and experience new levels of freedom as a result. It will benefit your relationship with yourself, with God, with your friends, with your family and, possibly down the line, in a romantic relationship too. If you're only motivated to do this because you think it will maximize your chances of a successful marriage, then quite frankly that's a shame. You're worth it either way.

Something vital to flag up: if you're waiting until you've fixed your brokenness before you date, you've taken a vow of celibacy. You are broken. This side of eternity, we are all going to struggle. You may tackle one thing only to realize there's another gaping character defect you now need to address somewhere else in your life. Married people reassure me that being in a couple reveals issues they never knew they had. I have a friend who has now been married for six years and the first year of her marriage was horrific. She told me she got married at one of the darkest points of her life. She had struggled with anxiety and hit a new low just after her wedding. Did it mean she'd got the timing wrong? Was she not supposed to be in a relationship until this was fixed? Not at all. Her husband was and is loyal and supportive and they waded through it together. Although, vitally, she didn't rely on him to fix her, she relied on God.

One thing I have done, and do genuinely back, is the idea of taking a break from dating – although if I hear anyone describe it as a 'season of singleness', I may throw up a little in my mouth. When you go into recovery from an addiction, it is recommended that you don't change your relationship status for a year. I was single and remained single for the duration of that time. Later down the line, I listened to a series of podcasts, *Sex, Love & God* (2013) by the First Evangelical Free Church of Fullerton (somewhere in the States) and felt God give me the nudge to take another break of six months. Since then, if I feel a bit bruised or exhausted by dating, I'll take a month or so off to top up. Earlier this year, I wholeheartedly threw myself into an initiative I have dubbed, 'No-Man Jan'.

It's also something I recommend to some of the women I mentor. One of those was Amy. Amy found herself caught up in a holiday romance with a man she knew had a girlfriend. She agreed to take a step back while we took a look at what had got her to that place. She said: 'When it was suggested that I had a six-month dating break, the idea terrified me. What if the love of my life came into my life at exactly that time? I prayed about it, spoke to a few friends and knew that that fear alone was reason enough to do it.'

The first merit of stepping back from dating is that it takes the power out of it. If you're afraid of timelines or being alone or never meeting anyone, it can take up a huge amount of your headspace. You can claim back your single time by locking it in for a while. This means actively turning down dates. Two weeks after taking the plunge, Amy got a message from a friend who wanted to set her up with a good-looking Christian lawyer he'd met at a party (classic) but, despite the desert-style temptation, she stuck to her guns and said no.

The break also means stepping away from dating apps or attending any singles events. It means not evaluating every person you meet for their dating potential. It means not checking everyone's finger for a ring. It means putting all that on pause (some of it you'll hopefully never pick up again anyway).

For people for whom their relationship status has become over-whelming, it means they can rest. I've heard a few people (John Mark Comer (2017) being one of them) say: 'If you worship romance and sex, you will always feel alone. Just as if you worship beauty, you will always feel ugly.' The more something (that isn't God) is your focus, the more damage it can do. Amy said: 'I'd felt for a long time that I was "ready" to meet the right person. But during that time I realized that I wasn't and was attracted to and attracting unavailable men, who would never be right for me. That realization helped me to get to the root of why that was and use tools to stop it happening again. Without having a dating break

I'm not sure I would have had the headspace to discover that and to move forward in a positive way.'

Don't listen to reports of people who took a year off dating and, within weeks of it ending, met their 'other half' and are now happily married with three kids and a Honda Odyssey. I'm not saying do this to find your partner; I'm saying do this to find yourself. If you're concerned that you're too old to waste time like that, then please don't be. It's not a waste of time. If you're getting that stirring inside you that this could be for you, then pray on it and take it seriously. God doesn't run out of time, remember?

At times, there can also be an undercurrent of prosperity gospel around the dating narrative. You may have been given the impression that if you do various things, God will bless you with an amazing partner, a happy marriage and a lifetime of mind-blowing sex. There are no guarantees. That is the painful truth. No one but God knows what's in store for you and every story is different.

I've spent time slating the pre-existing advice. But, as my tyrant first boss drummed into me: it's important to bring solutions, not problems. So how do you know when you're ready to date? Here are the questions I think you should ask yourself.

Have you culled the ex?

My friend Alex broke up with his long-term girlfriend a couple of years ago. Within a few months she had met someone else and, within a year of the break-up, while he was still healing, she was married. Hurt, he went to his church leaders to vent and ask for prayer. In the course of this conversation, he mentioned that he had some letters she had written to him and a book they were reading together. Without hesitation, the church leader encouraged him to rid himself of those reminders. She suggested he burn them. She even went as far as to provide him with a fireproof bucket and some matches to take to the park. Now Carlsberg don't do church leaders, but if they did . . .

I'm not saying you need to do an ex bonfire in the style of Alex or the girls from *Friends*. But it is important to emotionally let go of your ex and that often includes physically letting go of their stuff. If you're still harbouring his hoodie or her fancy shampoo then it's time for it to hit the bin/charity shop. After years of walking around wearing various ex-boyfriends' tracksuit bottoms to bed and T-shirts to the gym, I decided it was time to cull all relationship remnants. I chucked them out and went straight to the shops to get myself my own oversized men's clothes. To: me, from: me. That legendary day, I reclaimed my loungewear and strutted out of TK Maxx feeling like a queen.

But don't stop at clothes; a shoebox of memories, cards, presents, letters – if it's dragging you down, get rid. Log off their Netflix and pay for your own subscription. Unfollow on social media. Delete voicemails, WhatsApp conversations, emails and texts. You can't start the next chapter in your life if you're still thumbing through the last one. If this is filling you with dread, ask yourself why. Maybe you're not ready yet. That's fine. Take it easy and in time you'll get there. It will feel like shedding old skin.

Are you jealous of others in relationships?

How do you feel when you see another engagement announcement online? Is your immediate reaction to feel excited for the couple or do you take it personally that you're not there yet? Jealousy kills joy. I'm not standing on a high and mighty pulpit with this one – it is hard. But comparing other people's journeys with yours will only serve to make you feel low, rushed and panicked. Don't be someone who is so consumed by a craving for coupling-up that you can't attend an anniversary party or wedding. You'll miss out on so much. Things can get ugly when you start allowing jealousy to creep in. Have you ever said: 'If he can get a girlfriend, then I definitely should be able to.' Or thought: 'I'm way better looking than she is; how is she already married?' You've got to know that's wrong. They didn't volunteer their looks and character for your scrutiny just because they met someone they love. Conducting analyses like that takes vital brain power; it's exhausting. Give yourself a day off.

In situations that provoke a knee-jerk reaction, you can't help your first thought. But you can help your second. Active response: take captive that thought to make it obedient to Christ (2 Corinthians 10.5). Call it out and send it away using the tools from the Bible. Then pray a prayer of gratitude over that person/those people. This is the most effective response for tackling jealousy. If you can do that every time you get a pang of envy, your mindset will change very quickly and, eventually, so will that first thought. As Penelope Wilton's character said in Netflix series, *After Life* (2019): 'Happiness is amazing. It's so amazing it doesn't matter if it's yours or not.' Sometimes I have to remind myself of that.

Do you think you need to change your appearance?

When I asked Foo Fighters what one piece of advice they would offer to people dating, one spoke up immediately: 'People worry too much about how they look . . . Looks are important but not that important. What I want to know is, "Do I want to speak to them at the end of a long day?"' Are you planning on putting yourself out there once you've lost those 2 kg? Or bulked up to a certain weight? Do you think you need to wait till your skin clears up?

It's a balancing act because dating is based on attraction and a part of that is physical. So, it is important to be well presented, to have put thought into how you dress and to have good hygiene. But you don't need to fundamentally change how you look. I wish I could see you, so I could look you in the eye and tell you you look great.

Be careful deciding to change in aid of meeting a partner. You may need to remind yourself who you truly are in Christ. (That is: the son/daughter of a King. You are Royalty. Unsure? John 1.12, Galatians 3.26 and countless other references.) You may also have negative patterns to address, but who you ultimately are, the person who is trying (and failing at times) to do things well, who wants to be kind, to focus on what is right, to connect with people in a range of different ways – that person is good. You don't have to change for your future partner. You are you. God made you like that. He's working with you; he loves you an inordinate amount. When you look in the mirror and tell yourself you need to bulk up or lose weight or drink protein shakes or get lip injections to be ready to date, you're hurting him and you're hurting yourself.

Have you put being in a relationship in its rightful place?

How much emphasis have you put on meeting someone? Has it become all-consuming? Do you believe that if you could just meet someone, you'd be happy, your primary problem would be solved and your life could finally really start? If you're desperate for a relationship to sort things out for you, it may not be healthy for you to be in one right now. You could be Lenny. You may remember Lenny from *Of Mice and Men* (John Steinbeck, 1937) in GCSE English. Lenny liked soft things, so when he found a little mouse, he took it to pet, but in his enthusiasm, he smothered and killed it. You don't want to smother the mouse. Ask yourself what hole you believe a relationship will fill in your life and work out other, healthy ways to fill it. If a relationship comes after that it's a bonus.

Are you worried you have too much emotional baggage?

Emotional baggage? Oh, you mean the tough circumstances and pain you had to overcome to get where you are today? The difficulties God used to develop your character, tolerance, stamina and perseverance? The ones that developed your empathy so you could better connect with other people in their struggles? Take it from a former drug addict – carry the 'baggage' with your head held high and be grateful it got you where you are today. That's not a Primark wheelie carry-on, that's a Louis Vuitton valise set. It is beautiful.

Do you have an unhelpful pattern?

Pastor and author, Will van der Hart set up and runs The Dating Course out of London church, Holy Trinity Brompton. I went a few years ago with the intention of reliving my secondary school years by sitting in the back and mocking every second of it with friends. But, much to my disappointment, it was pretty good. He spoke about a pattern he had had in previous relationships, where he found himself dating a series of women with eating disorders: women who 'needed fixing'. If you've got a pattern of going for someone who needs a saviour, then you need to ask yourself why. As I once heard someone say at a conference: 'The position of Messiah has been filled'. Or maybe your pattern is writing things off too early? Being put off by superficial things? Panicking at the first signs things are getting serious? Or choosing people who are emotionally unavailable? If so, recognizing that pattern and taking some time to figure out why, could be a really valuable tool. This dovetails beautifully into my next question.

How much do you value yourself?

Do you realize what you're worth? Do you value yourself enough to only stand for the best and most respectful treatment from your partner? Is there a chance that low self-esteem could allow you to accept an abusive relationship? Are you ready to receive love? Are you ready to be truly known? Do you believe that when you expose the best and worst of yourself, someone will still love you? Will you try to get people to desire you rather than know and truly love you? These questions are big. When I work with women as their sponsor or through a mentoring scheme, this is what it usually boils down to. The source of it all.

If you don't know your value (the aforementioned royalty status), you can get in all kinds of trouble. The worst-case scenario, and one I frequently see on the Recovery Course, is that a lack of grounding in people's worth leads them to accept poor treatment in a relationship, or even abuse. If this is the case, then dating isn't safe for you right now. If that rings true for you, please seek help, speak to a counsellor, therapist, GP or your church leaders. Find someone you can confidentially be completely honest with.

Sometimes, that low self-esteem can be the result of the treatment a person has received at the hands of others or, in very serious cases, is the result of trauma. I'm going to talk about sexual abuse, rape and #metoo now, so if you're not in a place where you can read this, skip ahead to the next sub-heading. But if you possibly can, stay with me.

A 2013 report by the World Health Organization estimated that 35.6 per cent of women globally have experienced violence at the hands of their partner and/or non-partner sexual violence. In non-academic reports I've seen quoting that figure, they tend to round it to a nice neat 35 per cent. That 0.6 per cent represents the experiences of 2.25 million actual lives, so no rounding here. There are some suggestions that the figure could be nearer 70 per cent. The stats for men vary greatly from source to source, with some suggesting about 4 per cent of men experience sexual violence and others that that figure is closer to 16 per cent. If working on the Recovery Course has taught me anything, it's that assuming what happens in the world doesn't happen in the Church is naïve and dangerous. These statistics will be a reflection of the experiences of some people in the Church. They will be a reflection of the experiences of some of the people reading this book.

Please know this: you are so much greater than the sum of your negative experiences. Your value is infinitely more than what you have been shown. You are not to blame for your horrific treatment. It doesn't matter if you flirted, or got in the car, or made the wrong choice, or went on the wrong date, or went back to their house. If I am passed out on the floor with my wallet in my hand and a £50 note sticking out of it, does that mean the person who takes it hasn't committed a theft? Opportunity is not an excuse for crime. No one is ever asking for it. If you're not clear on that, please confide in someone and unpick the lies of the enemy. I implore you to speak to a professional. I won't go on as this isn't a book about processing trauma, but I wanted to speak that truth loud and clear.

Next, you need to know that dating after sexual abuse is nothing short of an act of bravery. I don't see a damaged, desperate person scrambling around for someone to love them. I see a soldier, who's been through the wars, who has clambered back up, and is now choosing to trust, to walk forward, to try. Love is the only war you win when you take off your armour and to do that after so much pain is brave. Your courage is inspirational. Know that you don't have to do anything. Be gentle with yourself and do what's right for you. Be careful with your choices and focus on people who are kind.

Don't let a fear of having to open up to a future partner about your experiences put you off dating. God's strength is in your weakness (2 Corinthians 12.9). There's never any need to unveil all your history immediately; you can discuss it when you're comfortable. When it comes to deciding what to share with someone, know that you're not doing it for approval. It's not so that they can add it to your evaluation sheet and decide if they want to be with you. It's because that is part of your story and, in time, you will choose to share it with them so they will know you a little bit better. It is a part of developing closeness. You owe no one anything.

Before we move on, I'm going to pray. I'm not there with you but if I were, this is what I'd do . . .

God, thank you that you are a God of justice. That your heart breaks at injustice. You hear the cries of those who have been harmed. You feel their pain. You know the damage that has been caused. I pray for your healing. That you would do something supernatural. That you would minister to the hurt, the pain that won't subside. That your presence, your peace and your Holy Spirit would fall on anyone who needs it, reading this right now. I pray for your strength in their weakness. I pray for your comfort and protection. And I pray for your restoration. Rebuild what has been broken; don't let them question their value. Let them feel and know your deep love. Amen.

Do you have capacity to handle a break-up?

Finally, and crucially, if you don't have the emotional and spiritual capacity to cope with a break-up, disappointment or rejection in a healthy way, you have no business dating right now. One of the All Saints said something poignant: 'My recent dating experiences have been really positive, even if I have been disappointed by some of the outcomes. But I think that's because I'm in a really good place.'

Dating can be brutal and you will never be unaffected by rejection. It's OK for it to be painful and for you to feel the pain. But if you're in a place where that pain could throw you off the rails, cause you to turn to unhealthy practices or drive you into a breakdown, then please be kind to yourself and give yourself some more time. The fact is that virtually everyone has experienced pain around romantic relationships. If you're single, every interaction, crush and dating experience before now has ended, bringing with it varying degrees of hurt. If you're going to do this and be fully present and vulnerable and open, there's no way of protecting yourself. There are no guarantees. Are you ready to potentially feel that way again? Do you have a good support network if the worst-case scenario should happen?

*

I hope this exploration has been helpful and encouraging for you. But please bear in mind that no one is ever really ready for anything. '*If you wait for perfect conditions, you will never get anything done*' (Ecclesiastes 11.4, TLB). Sometimes you've just got to jump. There may be very good reasons to wait (particularly if any of the above is applicable) but if there's nothing major – just a feeling that you're not sure – consider getting stuck in. You can take a break whenever you like. Don't waste time waiting for the certainty that no one ever feels anyway. Let's all be like those blokes everyone always talks about, who apply for jobs when they know they're only 60 per cent qualified. If you're waiting till you're 100 per cent ready, you probably should have already started.

The 'perfect' relationship

Thanks, Disney

Picture the scene: you're outside running an errand; maybe you're taking the bins out or cleaning your car in the street. The sun is blazing and you're in a great mood. Bolstered by the good weather, you start to sing to yourself. Maybe you've got Spotify on or the car radio's playing. Just as you're getting your groove on to Gaga, someone comes up behind you about a foot away and joins in with the song . . .

Startled, you stop singing and swing round to see the other half of your unsolicited duet. The other person also stops and says: 'Hello, did I frighten you?' Clearly concerned, you back away towards your house. The person continues: 'Wait, wait, please don't run away.' As you dash through the front door and slam it behind you, you hear your uninvited singing partner pick up the song where the two of you left off in an attempt to serenade you as you flee. Menacing, right? No one's stopping to swap numbers with the creepy crooner. Except this is the exact interaction between Snow White and Prince Charming in the Disney film (1937). Word for word. I sat through it to check. Did she call the police? Was she embarrassed and uncomfortable with his invasion of her personal space? Did she drop a message to the other princesses to tell them to watch out for the crackpot future king? None of the above. The next time we hear her speak about the prince, Snow White is talking to the seven dwarfs and explaining that she's 'in love with him', he's 'the only one' for her and 'there's nobody like him anywhere at all'. Those are *actual* quotes.

When the prince and Snow White are finally reunited, she is woken from her unconsciousness by his kiss and he leads her away, wordlessly, into the sunset. In the whole film Snow White doesn't say a word directly to the prince.

They never made a *Snow White 2*. Maybe that's because watching the slow and agonizing breakdown of a relationship that was entered into prematurely isn't very 'Disney'. I, for one, would pay to watch as Snow White grows to realize that marrying someone who looms up on young women and breaks into song isn't all it's cracked up to be; and as the prince gets fed up with all the woodland creatures leaving their droppings as they traipse through the house to help with all the various daily chores.

The relationships we saw as children to model our hopes and dreams on were fundamentally flawed. Rarely did feelings of love grow from a deep and mutual understanding of who the other was. It was an encounter that sparked love at first sight, followed by some questionable courtship practices. Belle was a hostage with Stockholm syndrome; Ariel changed her species and gave up her voice in order to gain favour with the prince; and Sleeping Beauty was given a non-consensual kiss while unconscious.

Instant attraction

We know all these are fairy stories, but the material we surround ourselves with has a tendency to stick, no matter how impervious we believe ourselves to be. Somewhere along the line we fell for the idea that instant attraction is preferable to that which builds and develops more slowly over a longer period of time. The reality is that some of the best, most fulfilling relationships don't kick off with irrepressible feelings of chemistry. In some cases, that chemistry wanes over time and in others it develops with greater engagement.

That said, establishing attraction is key before entering into a relationship with someone. But we could all be more open to the idea of finding that attraction somewhere unexpected or even with someone we've known for a while.

The best depiction of a healthy attraction I've heard is Will van der Hart's on The Dating Course. He compares a relationship to a church candle – one of those fat pillar ones. The attraction is the wick; you need it to get the thing going. But if you're all wick, you'll burn out quickly. The wax is the substance, the friendship, the deeper understanding of each other, the experiences you share. But if you're all wax, you can't get the flame going. However, if you have both, you've got a candle that will burn brightly and for a long time.

The one

You've found someone you connect with; you think there may be enough of that candle wax to keep the whole thing alight but you're not sure. How do you know that they're the one? How do you know when you've met your soulmate? Now this is key: they are neither 'the one' nor your 'soulmate'. Because neither of those things exist. Mr/Mrs Right is not out there. Get on with your life.

Back in the ancient days of Athens, Plato shared some questionable insight into the origin of humans. Turns out, way back when, people had four legs, four arms and a head with two faces. Zeus, despite being king of the gods, was afraid of what these eight-appendaged, double-faced people could do, so he split them down the middle. Humans, now incomplete, walked the earth pining for their other half, throwing their arms around each other and intertwining their bodies in an attempt to grow together. In summary, the idea of a missing person to complete you is not founded on any biblical truth. It's misinformation from Plato and *Jerry Maguire*. It is not a great premise to build your life and expectations on. It's a waste of time.

The fact is, there are a number of people you will meet in your life who would be a suitable marriage partner for you. You would have a different but fulfilling life with each. That person becomes 'the one' when you choose to commit to them, because you are making a promise to them to eliminate all others from the equation. Leaving just one.

The burden of choice

If you're intent on truly finding the best fitting jeans for you, you will have to try on every pair of jeans in the world before you know for sure you have identified the ideal ones. Even then, you will struggle to choose between the top handful of pairs as they all have their own unique merits. A more effective strategy is to shop around a bit, get a feel for what's on offer on your local high street and then choose a pair that's a decent fit. Jeans are never perfect, but you can find some you like and stick with them. The analogy gets a bit stuck after this because a pair of Levi's doesn't get the opportunity to choose you back, but you get my drift. I don't want to go down the rabbit hole of ranting about choice and modern culture, but I think we can all acknowledge that choice is every-where, like never before. But for some of us, the vast expanse of options is so overwhelming, we are crippled by a fear of making a decision we regret. I'm dubbing this 'privilege paralysis'.

Back in the day, when our parents or grandparents were deciding who to marry, there was far less dating. They just picked someone. Someone who could offer stability. A suitable match based on faith, geography and finances. These days we still want compatibility on those levels, but they also have to be our best friend. They have to dress well and get on with our friends and enjoy the same activities and not pronounce words weirdly and eat with their mouth closed and not smoke and be close (but not too close) with their family and be open to owning a dog at some point in the future.

In my years BC, I took myself off to The School of Life in North London for a seminar called 'How To Make Decisions'. The main take-away from the session was: the more options you have, the harder it is to choose. I continued researching, and not only do more options make it harder for you to choose but, according to Barry Schwartz's TED Talk, 'The paradox of choice' (2005), they also reduce your level of satisfaction with the choice you eventually make. This could mean that, having made a decision, when you realize that choice isn't absolutely perfect (and what in life is?), it's too easy to run through the array of options you turned down and imagine them to be superior. This regret retracts from the option you went for, whether it was good or not. Barry Schwartz explains this is because the more options you have, the higher your expectations for the one you pick.

Expectations are a killer. In recovery, we say 'expectations are resent-ments in the making'. Perhaps it's time to be realistic and take another look at the options you have rather than expanding your database. With this in mind, here's your challenge: if you had no way of meeting anyone new and adding to your pool of potential suitors – who would you ask out? Pop a bookmark in this page and drop them a line . . .

Idolatry of romance: love addiction

Is love addiction a thing?

MEGAN: There's no doubt in my mind that love addiction is real. I wouldn't say that I was a year and a half 'sober' from love addiction if I didn't truly believe that. I was consumed by the idea that I had to have someone else there so I wouldn't be alone. It's drummed into us as children that you're not successful if you don't have a house, a husband, a child and a good job. I felt like, if I didn't have one of those things, there was something wrong with me. I believed that if I met someone, all my problems would be shared. If I had someone there, suddenly I would be OK. In every new relationship I got these tremendous highs. I felt like this was finally going to be it. I would say things like, "It's you and me against the world" and, "You're my everything". I honestly thought all the issues we had would be OK if we were together. The deeper I went with that person, the more I felt like I was on a high. I would share my inner-most thoughts, knowing this is the person I'll be with for the rest of my life. I'll never be alone. I'll never have to experience loneliness or pain. There'll always be someone there . . .

There's serious debate in the field of addiction research about whether or not behavioural addictions should be classified as addictions at all. Gambling was only added to the addictions section of the *Diagnostic and Statistical Manual of Mental Disorders* (DSM) in 2013 with the release of DSM5, when previously it had been listed within impulse control disorders (T. Sztainert, 2017). The dilution of the term 'addiction' and the assigning of the stigma associated to it are both good reasons to be wary of applying it too liberally. If we're talking in spiritual terms, addiction is idolatry at its most extreme.

That said, there is compelling evidence that love can generate the same feelings of obsession and craving as a drug like cocaine. In one

2010 neuroimaging study (H. E. Fisher and others), researchers showed subjects a photograph of a person they had recently been rejected by, but who they reported they were still intensely in love with. Viewing this image activated areas of the brain associated with gains and losses, cocaine craving, addiction and emotional regulation. They suggested that the activation of areas involved in cocaine addiction could explain the obsessive behaviours associated with rejection in love.

There's also suggestion that love addicts can relapse in the same way a drug addict can (H. E. Fisher and others, 2016). Long after the end of a relationship, they can be triggered by a song, memory, person or event that can initiate craving, obsessive thinking and, in some cases, compulsive calling or showing up in the hope of rekindling the relationship. Along the same lines, there is research highlighting the similarities between addiction and stalking (J. R. Meloy and H. Fisher, 2005).

Whether or not this obsessive and compulsive pattern can be labelled an 'addiction', is – in my opinion – just a question of semantics. The fact is, the feelings Megan experienced (and the neurological pathways underpinning them) are very real. Unlike drugs, which, as a poison, can lead to death, love addiction is unlikely to kill you, but it will stop you living.

What are the characteristics of love addiction?

MEGAN: Everyone's story is different but I found myself in a string of damaging, toxic and abusive relationships. I was never on my own. I always jumped into the next relationship without healing from the last. I would be so deeply in love with each person. But it would always go from a whirlwind romance to a living nightmare and then I would be stuck. When things turned, I just couldn't understand why this was happening to me again. I didn't understand what I was doing wrong. But no matter how bad a relationship got, I felt the idea of losing that person and being on my own was worse than the pain of staying. I slowly let my standards slip and would tolerate worse and worse behaviour from my partners. I was so addicted to the person and so consumed by what I thought that person would bring to my life, that I thought I couldn't leave. Letting go of the fantasy I had built up of our relationship was too painful. In order to avoid being alone, I would take back exes who had cheated on me or beaten me up. My friends told me I was obsessed and I would make men my world. As soon as a new guy was on the scene, all my attention was diverted on to them. That in itself was exhausting. I never felt like anything I did was good enough.

There are no universally recognized definitions or diagnostic criteria for 'love addiction' (M. Reynaud and others, 2010) and characterizing an addiction is difficult, as it can play out in different ways depending on the individual and that person's experience. However, there is a diagnostic questionnaire, Mark Falango's 'Love addiction self-assessment questionnaire' (LASA) (2012), which is used by clinicians and is readily available online. This is adapted from the '40 Questions for self-diagnosis' (1985) from Sex and Love Addicts Anonymous (SLAA). Both these evaluation tools consider how feelings of love have affected a person's emotional state, their behaviour and their beliefs.

There is a danger that people can read a list of criteria and diagnose themselves as hopeless cases. If you're going to google either questionnaire and quiz yourself, then bear in mind that everyone to a certain extent displays signs of codependency. Love is a strong emotion and elicits a strong response. That said, if you find yourself relating to a large proportion of the criteria, it may be worth doing some additional research and reaching out to a few people who have experienced love addiction themselves (more on that to follow).

How do you prevent love addiction?

MEGAN: I think there's a correlation with people growing up in dysfunctional households and developing love addiction. Because people learn to caretake within their relationships. I grew up in an alcoholic home and it meant that I craved stability. Home was never safe. I thought if I found someone, they would fill that need to be loved and the need to feel wanted. But actually, what I found was a series of unstable and incredibly painful relationships that replicated what was going on at home. The way I had been shown love was abusive, so therefore if someone showed me abuse in a relationship, that was normal; that was love. I had a lot of self-doubt and trauma to work through to stop me latching on to another person.

Researchers suggest that love addiction is likely to have manifested by the time a person reaches adolescence (S. Sussman, 2010). Some recommend using drug and alcohol addiction-prevention techniques as a suitable strategy (S. Sussman, 2017), while others suggest that lowering the prevalence of love-addiction normative beliefs could make a difference (S. Sussman, 2020). This includes challenging statements like, 'anything is possible with love' or preventing the reinforcement of the idea that stalking someone you love is normal behaviour. We can all be taking steps to challenge the normative beliefs that are detailed in the scientific research. You may think the research on stalking is too extreme to be relevant to yourself or anyone you know, but what about cyber stalking? Have you laughed with friends about incessantly googling someone? Or have you challenged that as a destructive behaviour pattern? Are you normalizing or standing against it? Enhancing self-esteem and encouraging people to avoid impulsive situations around love and see how these are actually incongruent with their future aspirations, as well as stress and mood management, have been suggested as helpful tools in addressing love addiction (S. Sussman, 2020). Researchers have even suggested that warning labels on TV and film that differentiate between 'love fiction' and 'love fact' may be beneficial in preventing such an addiction (S. Sussman, 2020).

When Megan refers to a chaotic home life as a risk factor, she's basing this on her experience rather than using stats and figures, but everything I've seen tells me she is right. I have met and worked with countless children of addicts or people from unstable home environments, who have to work through issues around love addiction and codependency, possibly due to the lack of healthy relationships and boundaries they had modelled for them. A chaotic homelife is a risk factor for so many addictions and mental health problems. I'll discuss ways we, as a church family, can be pulling together as a community to combat this later on in the book, but if you know someone growing up in a situation like this, ask yourself how you can be a stabilizing or comforting influence for that person. It could make all the difference.

What does sobriety look like for love addicts?

MEGAN: I found the process of getting sober _____ing awful. But it was the most rewarding thing I've ever done. It was so freeing. My last abusive relationship coincided with the Recovery Course. It was the first time I'd decided to be single and to actually face the addiction. It was like stripping myself bare. You're just alone with yourself. Your self-esteem is so low and the fact that you're alone in the quiet just affirms all the negative things you think about yourself. I didn't believe I deserved someone who treated me well. It was a learning process. I had to learn to handle rejection and not take it personally. I had to learn to go on dates and not picture our children or, after we'd kissed, picture how he was going to propose. I had to learn to take it one date at a time. It was tough to stop making men the centre of my universe. I was chained to my phone and social media and I never realized. I wouldn't make plans with people in case the person I was interested in wanted to do something. I was always making sure I was available for that person, just in case. Going through the process of recovery has given me so much freedom in areas I didn't even know I needed freedom. I didn't realize I was in pain because I'd lived like that for so long, it had just become normality. But now I know I am no less of a person because I am single.

Psychologist, Eric Griffin-Shelley, details the aims of his work in establishing long-term sobriety for love addicts in his book *Sex and Love: Addiction, treatment and recovery* (1997). He explains that he encourages service users to become less defensive, detailing how this allows them to be more open to developing genuine intimacy, affirmation and self-knowledge. He also helps them to eliminate masks and unhealthy attitudes and develop a stronger, more authentic sense of self. This ultimately is designed to allow them to get what they've wanted all along: meaningful connections with others.

On a practical level, when working through love addiction with people on the Recovery Course, we start by identifying behaviours that are unhealthy but also healthy practices they could be replaced by. In the short term, guests are encouraged to avoid the unhealthy practices and use the healthy ones to foster a lifestyle they're proud of. When it gets difficult to uphold these principles (which it inevitably does), we encourage people to use the 'tools' of recovery to help them stay strong. These are things like: phone calls with other recovering addicts, prayer, the Bible, accountability and 12-step fellowships. We then work through the 12 steps with those people, which is a process of handing control to God, taking an inventory of where our lives have gone and handing unhealthy patterns to him, making amends where we've been wrong and maintaining these principles going forward.

What we're working towards for people is freedom; a life where they are no longer consumed by the idea of love and marriage and romance and sex. A lot of people can't imagine what life is like when they're not handing over their freedom to the opinion of and attention from someone they're attracted to. We hope every person we work with will be able to develop healthy relationships over time, with God at the centre.

I think I might be addicted to love. What should I do?

MEGAN: I really found the 12-step fellowship [Sex and Love Addicts Anonymous] helpful. At first, I didn't think I was a love addict; I thought everyone else was the problem. It was just that I'd had a 35-year run of bad luck. Identifying with other people was my real 'eureka!' moment. I realized that (a) I wasn't alone and (b) there was help I could access without jumping through hoops. I found Melody Beattie's book, *Codependent No More* (2018) and Pia Mellody's, *Facing Love Addiction* (2003) really helpful, along with podcasts and audiobooks and forums. We are so blessed with what we have available online now. The only other thing I would say is, just don't give up. Recovery from this is so worth it. Facing love addiction is really painful but it is the most rewarding emotional sobriety you can obtain.

As with any addiction, there are mechanisms for coping with the chronic and the acute symptoms. Researchers suggest that if a love addict has recently been rejected, they should focus on staying busy with novel, healthy activities (these release dopamine and create feelings of energy and optimism) (S. Sussman, 2020). Physical exercise is also cited as being helpful (H. E. Fisher, 2017). In order to address the chronic symptoms, group and individual therapies are recommended (S. Sussman, 2020) and psychotherapy is often cited as the cornerstone of the treatment of love addiction, but its efficacy has not been properly investigated (M. Sanches and V. John, 2019).

No matter how you choose to address it, there are three things you should know. First, you are not alone. I hope Megan's story has shown you that. There are countless other people out there who have felt how you feel and who have found recovery. Second, you can recover. God loves you as you are, but he loves you too much to leave you as you are. I've watched as people have battled some horrific addictions, but freedom is there for those who claim it. It's there for you. Finally, the strongest thing I've ever heard anyone say is: 'Help me.' I don't know anyone who has worked through an addiction alone. Reach out to members of your church, get yourself on a Recovery Course or Steps Programme or Celebrate Recovery Course. Attend a local SLAA meeting. Make sure you have people who are praying for you. Whatever you do, reach out and ask for help. Bring this out into the light and do it with a team around you. There are so many people who want to help.

Part 2
UP TO DATE

I kissed dating hello

I want to make one thing really clear: single people don't have to date. They don't have to want to meet someone. They can be content being single for a while or be content being single full stop. If, however, you've made a decision not to date out of fear – of rejection, of exposing yourself or of 'putting yourself out there' – then that may be something you want to circle back to. The safest thing is not to try. The safest thing is to pretend you never wanted it in the first place. But if you choose to take the plunge and try out dating – whether for the first time or the one hundred and first – I hope this section will be helpful to you.

There is no dating in the Bible – probably because the concept did not exist in biblical times. This means, as with many things, we have to rely on the application of biblical principles to modern practices. It means we're liable to get it wrong.

In 1997, a 21-year-old American wrote a Christian book called *I Kissed Dating Goodbye* (Joshua Harris), its central idea being that dating should be avoided. Friendships should be formed and when a man is certain he wants to pursue marriage with a woman, he should then begin courting her (this involves asking parental permission to court and going on chaperoned dates). The book calls for moral and sexual immaculacy on the part of the men and women involved and recommends only kissing your partner for the first time on your wedding day. It advises that any intimacy you experience with partners before they are your husband/wife involves giving a part of your heart away, and suggests that you will carry this baggage to the altar with you. The book changed the game for single Christians as churches handed it out to members of their congregation and put pressure on people to uphold its principles. This resulted in people being terrified to show interest in someone without being absolutely certain they wanted to marry them. It meant that when someone was asked out, the invitee assumed the asker had already decided on working towards a wedding.

I could systematically pick this apart, but in light of a 2018 documentary by the author, Joshua Harris, renouncing the ideas outlined in the book, I'm not going to; he came across as a really good bloke. Regardless, there are elements of his once-promoted narrative that I believe have crept down to the attitude in the Church today: the expectation that a quick breakfast could lead to a lifetime of breakfasts in bed; the fear that someone will have blended your two names within ten minutes of you asking them out . . .

Often, the big expectations are attributed to the women and the fear to the men, although in my experience this playing field is far more level. For some people, there's also a fear of flirting. People are keen to keep things friendly and not to sexualize interactions but there must be a way two people can signal interest in conversation without risking a scarlet A. In Neil Strauss's book, *The Game* (2007), a pick-up artist teaches his socially inept mentees to identify 'indicators of interest' (IOIs) in their targets (that is, the women they want to manipulate into having sex with them). This book may be full of utter _____ but I do think there's something Christians could take from the IOIs. If more people used them to signal attraction and more people knew how to pick up on them, I think we'd get a lot more people feeling confident enough to make a move and ask someone for a coffee. These IOIs include: turning your body to face the person, tilting your head as you talk, eye contact, laughing, a light touch on the arm and mirroring body language. It's basic. But so many people don't bother reverting to these classic cues, instead favouring passivity.

My feeling is, like many other people I spoke to while working on this book, it's time to take dating a lot less seriously. Just go and get some coffee. Don't tell your life story or ask whose family they want to spend Christmas with. Just get coffee. Don't pack your heart up in a little box and present it at the table. Don't panic that you should be doing this perfectly and worry you're not 'guarding their heart'. You've really only got to have a coffee. Don't expect or even plan for a second date. It's just a _____ing coffee.

If you're thinking, I see all that, but accepting a coffee with more people sounds like a lot of time and a huge caffeine intake, I hear you. But the fact is, if you want to meet someone, you're going to have to put in the groundwork. You don't pray to God for a house without looking online. You don't pray for a job but never send out your CV. This is the same. Don't pray for a partner without doing some of the legwork yourself.

Will it be fun? At times maybe, other times not. In *How I Met Your Mother*, the character Barney Stintson says there should be an off-ramp 15 minutes into a date: an opportunity for you both to call it early doors, because when you know, you know. In a world where other people's feelings don't matter, I would totally agree and I would have used this slip road regularly. The fact is, we have to do better than that, so when you're on a date that's a bust – much like when the battery dies on your electric toothbrush mid-clean – you're there anyway, so you might as well just push on.

One piece of advice I found helpful came from author and podcaster, Pandora Sykes. She said her dating experience was just bad until it was good. This binary model for dating will not ring true with everyone but it serves as an encouragement for me. Because even if it's bad, it doesn't mean you're not making progress. There's no gradient or shades of grey. It's just bad, until you meet someone who makes it good.

Dating through the ages: a to-do list

2000 BC

- Wait till Father identifies you as ready for a wife.

- Have Father send his servant to preferred wife-finding region.

- Have servant swear oath to bring you back a wife.

- Pray for God to send an angel ahead to prepare future wife.

- Send servant with ten camels loaded to the brim with treasures.

- Once servant reaches agreed territory, he should identify a good well.

- Servant will settle at aforementioned well towards evening, when women will be drawing water.

- Servant to pray for wisdom to identify right woman.

- Servant to ask potential wife to share her water so that he can drink; if she also offers water for camels, she is the one.

- When camels have finished drinking, servant to present woman with a gift of a nose ring and two bracelets.

- Servant to ask to stay in her home.

- When she agrees, servant should worship God for this blessing.

- Servant to ask woman's father if she can come back with him.

- When he agrees, worship God some more.

- Servant to present her with more gold and jewellery and give further gifts to her mother and brother.

- Servant to then hurry back with soon-to-be wife, not allowing for any hold-ups.

- While waiting for servant, go out to a field to meditate; this will be perfectly timed with the arrival of servant and new wife (keep fingers crossed that you and your dad's servant agree on what constitutes a beauty).

- Breathe a sigh of relief when you finally meet bride as, although veiled, you like the look of her.

- Take her to meet Mum.

- Get married.

AD 1950

- Wait till 18 years old.

- Survey pool of suitors in immediate area: start with church, school, street and expand to wider neighbourhood if necessary.

- Identify an attractive girl.

- Ascertain that your parents would be happy with her, that she is from a good family and goes to church.

- Call girl at home, navigating awkward introductory conversation with her dad.

Dating through the ages: a to-do list

- Ask if she would like to go for dinner and then to a church dance.

- Make sure you can afford to pay for said dinner.

- Collect girl from home; politely introduce yourself to parents so they can see you're not crazy.

- At dinner, ensure you pull out seat for her, ask what she would like to eat and order on her behalf.

- Pay for dinner.

- Meet with other friends on dates at church dance; make sure everyone knows the two of you have come together so no one tries to 'cut in'.

- Impress her with your lindy hop.

- Walk her home and ensure she is back by time specified by parents; ask for a second date on walk.

- After a handful of similar outings, ask if she would like to 'go steady' and seal the deal with a cheap ring.

- Continue dating in a group setting.

- Introduce her to your family to ensure they are happy with the match.

- Spend time with her family to ensure they are also happy.

- Within a year, approach her dad and ask his permission to propose to her – hope he says yes.

- Propose – hope she says yes.

- Get married.

AD 2020

- Wait till 30 years old or till enough of your friends have got married to apply some pressure – whichever comes first.

- Ask friends to set you up with someone, download apps and start scouring the pews in your church/desks in your office/commuters on the Tube.

- Worry that all the good ones have gone.

- Finally identify someone you find attractive.

- Establish a means of contacting person privately through a dating app/Facebook Messenger/direct messaging/extracting phone number from a WhatsApp group set up for a mutual friend's surprise birthday.

- Send person a non-committal small-talk message.

- Once you've received a reply, send another slightly more flirtatious message.

- Buoyed by yet another speedy response, message asking to meet for a drink (don't specify it as a date so you have plausible deniability if the answer is no).

- Check phone at 90-second intervals.

- Put phone to one side and resign yourself to not going near it till later that evening.

- Check phone again 18 minutes later.

- When you still haven't had a reply that evening, check the person's social media to verify if there has been other phone-based activity.

- When you still haven't heard back the following day, run through a number of scenarios where the person has fallen down a well on a run and broken a leg – consider contacting his or her sibling/friend/pastor to set up a search party and deploy Lassie.

- Abandon all SOS messages and tell Lassie to stand down when you eventually get a response 21.5 hours after your message.

- Wait 22 hours to respond (in defiance) and then set up the drink.

- Rampantly google person to ensure he or she actually is as attractive as you think, has friends, a regular social life, hasn't committed any crimes or been a guest on Jeremy Kyle.

- Arrive ten minutes late for drink so as not to appear too keen.

- Enjoy evening, rolling out some of your favourite lines, like comparing Uber ratings and making them guess your actual age.

- Perform ritual hand dance over the bill before agreeing to 'go Dutch'.

- Say you'd like to go for another date as you round off the first.

- Follow up with a series of messages the next day, always waiting slightly longer than they did to reply.

- Secure second date and follow up with a third and fourth.

- After three months of unspecified but almost certainly exclusive dating, ask if datee will be your boyfriend/girlfriend.

- Begin process of introducing to friends and eventually family.

- After two years, put in a cursory call to boyfriend/girlfriend's parents to say you intend to propose, in the name of politeness and tradition, but knowing full well you will ask whether you get their blessing or not.

- Propose – hope for a yes.

- Get married.

Caught out there: Christian v. secular dating

Theoretically, Christians should have an advantage when it comes to matters of the heart. Aside from having the ultimate handbook for life, complete with clear instructions on how to treat others, we also have a model of perfect love in God. God is love (1 John 4.8) and love is patient, kind, non-envious, not boastful or proud (1 Corinthians 13.4–8) – you remember, from the last wedding you were at?

So why, when I put a shout-out on social media, did I get a story from one Christian woman who no longer feels comfortable dating Christian men? Why did a survey (2014) conducted by Samuel Verbi at mega church, Holy Trinity Brompton invite somebody to respond, 'I've had more lovely/respectful dates on Tinder/Happn in the past six months than in three years at my church. I honestly wish I'd joined them sooner'? Why did one of All Saints share that she's considered dating outside church on multiple occasions, because she finds the people more straightforward about what they want and therefore gets far more offers of dates? Why do a lot of my male friends start dating out of the church to avoid the 'high expectations and pressure'?

As I dug around for more information, reports came back of Christian dating where people were made to feel inadequate, being dropped and picked up when it suited their date. One person told me the guy she dated would ignore her as punishment if she did something 'non-biblical'. She then explained that the whole thing ended when they got drunk together, had sex and he cut ties with her as she was clearly 'unchristian'. She has since found a kind, non-Christian man, who is attentive to her and respects her faith, despite not sharing it. And quite frankly, who can blame her? I feel the rage erupting out of me just relaying that story. It's like a warning-sign scenario from *The Handmaid's Tale* (Margaret Atwood, 1985). It's not just men; there are also women who have subjected their partners to this kind of confused, double-standard, pathetic pseudo-holiness. I have heard stories left, right and centre; all judgemental, all demanding superhuman standards when clearly failing to live up to them themselves.

Dating in the Church: the big issues

The fact is, there is a lot of pressure on people in the Church to be perfect. Women can feel inferior as men search for the woman of Proverbs (Proverbs 31.10–31). It can appear as though men want a woman they find physically attractive, but women can't make attempts to attract men with their appearance, instead needing to look demure; not sexy but pretty. Incidentally, this is the same instruction given to a rape victim who takes the stand to testify against an attacker.

Men can feel pressured to take the lead, have sound, wise judgement and 'direct' their partner in spiritual matters. Even in this modern age, they can feel obliged to be able to single-handedly financially support themselves, their partner and any additional family members who may come along. I have one friend who didn't want to propose to his girlfriend because he wasn't in a position to send any theoretical future children to private school. As if that was (a) a prerequisite for spawning offspring and (b) his sole financial responsibility.

The pressure to date in the Church can be overwhelming. Caring enquirers can show you misplaced sympathy when you tell them you're not seeing anyone. They can scrabble around to pair you off with anyone who is also single and vaguely the same age. You can be written off as picky if you don't find a connection with their chosen match. One of the guys in Foo Fighters told me: 'I get cornered by the older women in my church to ask why I'm not asking out more girls, as if it's a war effort and I'm not doing my part.'

While we're on the topic of pressure, as a Christian with the end goal of dating always being marriage, there is immense pressure to get it 'right'. There's a reluctance to 'suck it and see' (horrific choice of idiom in a dating chat, but don't get distracted by it). Trial and error is frowned upon because the stakes are so high, but if you don't give it a go, you won't know.

If you do decide to date someone in church and it doesn't work out, much like dating at work, you then have to see that person on Sundays and at midweek events. There's no escaping your ex. But you're Christian, so are expected to deal with it with grace, patience and endurance, when all you want to do is ball up your hymn sheet and lob it at the back of their head. This often causes people to move church, to have to uproot themselves from the community they've invested in and start again – a high price for six dates that went a bit south. But the final and most commonly cited issue with dating in the Church is the stark gender imbalance. There are twice as many single women as there are men, leaving two women to battle it out over each empty chair when the music stops. The heightened competition means men can, at times, feel pounced on by women on a 'husband-hunt'.

I've got a single friend who is a bit of a box-ticker. If you're looking for dating capital, he's got it and it doesn't go unnoticed. I can anticipate the moment a woman will sidle up to me and ask for an introduction. I've been asked to set him up so often, I'm his unofficial romantic PA. I also have female friends who, in the outside world, would illicit the same effect, but in church stand out less due to the abundance of options.

This gender imbalance is explored extensively by Samuel Verbi following his survey at HTB. He explains that the lack of men creates frustration, as women feel there aren't enough opportunities and men are frustrated by the level of intensity associated with dating. The resulting phenomenon, he says, is that there are low levels of commitment and defined dating in church communities but high levels of emotional intimacy between sexes. Interestingly, he cites research that suggests the same can be reported in other groups with fewer men than women, like some college campuses or some African American communities (where one in seven of the men is in prison). Verbi observes that women will often feel led on by these relationships where no one ever defines the interaction as a date but emotional intimacy is shared. For the men in church, this can also have an ugly side effect. Some of my male friends will happily admit they expect their future wife to be better looking than they are. Why is that? Because they can. Because the dice are weighted in their favour. Verbi comments that the lack of investment from men could be due to their perception of the diminishing value of women due to the flooded market. He said: 'If Christian men perceive they can achieve a particular standard, all standards below this perception will be subconsciously no longer as attractive.'

My interpretation of this has always been that people who need to 'date up' in this way are harbouring insecurities and are looking to be validated by their partner. Here, a 10/10 wife does for insecurity what an expensive car does for a small penis (I'm typing this with a smile as I'm pretty sure my editor will delete it immediately).[1] Verbi also observed that, once a Christian man has chosen a partner, he is likely to feel less satisfied with that choice than he would in a balanced market.

Advice for all genders: if you're going to have a checklist for a future spouse and if you insist on putting looks on that list, you are wrong to expect your partner to have something you can't match. If you want a ten but you're a six, you need to ask yourself some questions – or at the very least get down the gym.

Dating outside the Church isn't easy either, but at least you're not confined to such a small pool. If you decide to drop the faith requirement for your dates, this opens up a large number of potential mates. Plus, as All Saints pointed out, women often find the calibre of people showing an interest in them higher and the attention often more consistent and sincere than that of the men in church. There are plenty of people who would also say they find secular dating less pressurized and, sadly, the people kinder.

Should you date non-Christians?

There are arguments for dating non-Christians. Not least the ones above. Plus, just having your faith in common with the person you're dating does not mean you're on the same page. You can have as many differences with another Christian as you can a non-Christian.

There are also strong arguments not to. 2 Corinthians 6.14 says: 'Don't become partners with those who reject God. How can you make a partnership out of right and wrong? That's not partnership; that's war. Is light best friends with dark?' (MSG). We've all heard it, although you've probably heard the non-*Message* version that talks about being 'unevenly yoked'. Aside from potentially creating conflict, it would be a large part of your life that you keep separate and can't fully share with your partner. They wouldn't pray with you when something goes wrong. They won't *fully* understand your commitment to God and Jesus. They will be exercising their own judgement in situations rather than deferring to the Bible. Without this, even with the best will in the world and

---

1 I'll let you have this one, Lauren.

a solid sense of justice and morality, people will never be able to achieve the insight of God in difficult situations. They won't be working towards the same ideals and biblical standards. You would be, quite literally, singing from a different hymn sheet. That said, when my mum and dad met, she went to church weekly and my dad didn't. If she had decided he wasn't 'Christian enough', my sister and I wouldn't be here. And I have a number of friends who converted to Christianity after dating someone who introduced them to faith. This, however, I believe to be less common than the scenario where someone dates a non-Christian and gradually becomes less committed to faith and church.

I don't want to tell you that dating a non-Christian is wrong because I don't think it's a one-size-fits-all situation. But I do think it's important that your dating life doesn't interfere with your faith and Christian principles and, instead, encourages them to grow and deepen. If you're not finding that with your partner, Christian or otherwise, then maybe it isn't right for you.

Lonely hearts would like to meet

WLTM – Christian woman

Christian man WLTM fun, laid-back, Jesus-loving woman with whom there is an instant and sustained spark throughout the duration of our relationship. Partner must be immediately identifiable as sexually attractive to both myself and my friends without attempting any seduction or wearing clothes that are even slightly revealing. Sexually inexperienced, excellent kisser. Facially attractive, without too much make-up. No fake tan or sunbeds. Mustn't try too hard. Well-kept and in good shape ideal, not due to shallowness but as this would be most compatible with my active lifestyle (and the doors in my flat are atypically slim). Ideally pitch and volume of voice low and pleasing at all times. Extensive reader but tempered when expressing own opinion (happy to be deferred to if ever unsure). Radicals, feminists and boat-rockers need not apply. Generally relaxed and laid-back attitude, not too demanding of time or resources. Highly skilled in hospitality, able to cheerfully entertain a group of my friends (preferably with catering). Tolerates sport silently and with mid-level of enjoyment that also allows for post-match conversation. Faith of paramount importance despite being the last thing mentioned. Will be heavily involved in church ministry, either taking a children's group at the family service or lending her angelic voice to backing vocals in the worship band (instrument negotiable, provided not percussion or guitar). Please don't reply to this directly as I don't find women who make the first move attractive.

WLTM – man of God

Devoted Christian WLTM faith-filled partner with whom there is a connection on a deeply spiritual level. GSOH essential, able to hold own at the dinner table and in a room of friends, who will be scrutinizing his every move and ranking him on a scale of zero to husband-material. Must not crack under pressure. Must be keen member of a church that is not too liberal or conservative. Must pray passionately, enjoy worship (but not too loudly or out of key) and put his hands up on rare occasions when really moved by the Spirit. Worship leaders will be prioritized. Looks not important but expected that body shape reflects the extensive level of exercise he enjoys. Running, cycling and two to three Iron Mans a year preferable. Men under 5 foot 6 inches need not apply. Need not be rich, although pay cheque will be in line with his position in a career that he has been passionately pursuing since leaving university (with at least a 2:1 in a sensible degree). Will be focused and driven on said career while not letting it spill over into his private time and not speaking about it too much on dates. Homeowner preferable but can rent if living with agreeable housemates and home doesn't feel too 'studenty'. Those still living with parents need not apply. Won't self-identify using the word 'feminist' but will subscribe to the majority of its associated principles. Won't expect a woman to take sole responsibility for cooking, cleaning and child-rearing, but will still adhere to the 'women and children on the lifeboats first' rule if we were ever on a cruise that went awry. I'm based in SW11 but happy for you to travel to me if based further afield.

Who to date?

Let go of 'your type'

When I lived in France for two and a half years, all I met was French men. When I first got there, I didn't find them attractive. French men tended to be shorter than British men; they spoke differently, gestured differently, dated differently. After a year, I couldn't imagine myself dating someone who wasn't French. Now I've been back in England for a few years and I'm firmly back on to British men: slightly less suave, slightly less romantic, slightly more Nando's.

'Your type' doesn't exist. It is just a product of your exposure. If you think you're not attracted to people of a certain race, then you probably don't hang around with people of that race enough. Open your mind and your social circle so you see people as individuals and not grouped by their skin colour/country of origin/job/any other characteristic. Once you humanize a group, you'll find people within that community who you're attracted to.

When it comes to looks, your type doesn't have to be smoking hot. It doesn't have to be someone other people would stop and look twice at in the street; or even someone your friends would agree is good-looking – as long as you find that person attractive. Once you let go of that ridiculous standard, you'll find attraction in more unexpected places. Plus, when it comes to looks, the most attractive person in the room is rarely the best-looking.

But having a type isn't all about looks. I've got friends with checklists as long as their arms of things they want in a partner: skills, hobbies, academic achievements. None of it matters if you connect well with someone. Scrap the whole lot. If they're kind, share your faith and you have great conversations, you're on to a winner. The rest is just cladding.

Let go of 'the people on the subs bench'

If you've got someone you message for a bit of a flirtation when you're between dates, someone you vibe with but you're not sure if it's enough to actually make it a thing, it's time to ask that person out or leave well alone. If you've got a deal that when you're both 40 you'll get married, just ask that person out now. If someone has enough credentials to consider for a relationship in the future and the two of you can flirt enough to make that pact, then there's enough going on for you to go on the date. Either you'll know for sure it's not a thing and can drop it or you can crack on with the relationship ahead of the allotted time and spend more years together. If you've got a friendship you're hoping will progress into something more, it's time to say so. Be brave. It's better to know either way.

Let go of 'chasing after the ones who aren't chasing after you'

Classic story: a friend of mine went on a date with someone the other day. They had a good time; he was pleasant and friendly, but she just wasn't excited by him. She couldn't say she fancied him. She was annoyed with herself because it would have been be so much easier if she did. He was kind and funny and interested in her, but something intangible just wasn't there for her. Should she date him anyway and see if it could progress? Despite having already spent a solid amount of time in his company, both one-to-one and in a group? My answer was no. She shouldn't force herself into a relationship with someone she wasn't attracted to; attraction is important and he would want to be with someone excited by him.

There is a phenomenon a lot of people recognize here: that the ones they fancy never fancy them and the ones they don't fancy are always interested. It's like indifference is a siren call. If that is a pattern for you, here are a few questions:

- Do you find it hard to be attracted to someone when you find out they're attracted to you?
- Do you feel the need to 'chase' or 'win' someone?

- If someone is attentive, does their availability make you feel they're not good enough for you?

If any of your answers to these questions is 'yes', it may be worth exploring what's going on there. Could it be self-punishment? Do you think you're not worthy of the attention? Are you looking for the thrill of the chase over the stability of a relationship?

If you identify this pattern, it doesn't mean you go back and start dating the last person who showed you attention, despite a lack of feelings. But maybe it means you ask God what's going on? Perhaps it means you ask him to open up your heart to the idea that you could be attracted to one of these people who is attracted to you? I asked my therapist about the idea of finding someone emotionally available to date. She said: 'It is of paramount importance that you find somebody who knows how to love. Somebody who will love you, not change you. You can have a beautiful object in front of you, but if you don't know how to paint, you're not going to make a masterpiece.'

Let go of 'the spark'

The spark is a myth created by pick-up artists and idiots. Feelings of attraction can be fostered with manipulation tactics, so people who are insecure and unvalidated in a relationship will mistake that anxiety for excitement. Suddenly, a whole host of people will only want to be in a relationship where they are ignored and badly treated because they've confused that with a mark of true connection. If you've read Neil Strauss's *The Game* (and hopefully you haven't), you will have come across tactics like 'negging' (the act of offering someone a backhanded compliment to undermine that person's confidence and increase desire for approval) and blowing hot and cold. Or maybe you've been victim of delayed responsiveness and deliberately promoting feelings of jealousy in a partner. The sad fact is that these approaches can be effective and some people play these games without even consciously deciding to do so. Be aware of these things, particularly if you've battled with low self-esteem, so when you see them, you can build up a resistance and run for the hills. Resist short-term fixes and hold out for supportive and edifying love.

It is true that you need to feel physically attracted to the person but that shouldn't be induced by feelings of uncertainty. It is also acceptable – no, preferable – for that romantic attraction to develop over time rather than being ablaze from the moment you lock eyes. If you have to manipulate or seduce someone into wanting you, you're not on the path to developing love. You're on the path to developing desire.

Mature love is not based on a spark or on a sexual desire associated with another person. To be desired is to be wanted for what you give someone: affirmation and gratification. It is to be viewed as a possession. Being accepted sexually is not the same as being loved. If love is intertwined with a person's most alluring qualities, it won't last. The things that draw us to a person sexually are repeatable; you can find them in a million other people. Love based solely on a spark is easily replaceable by someone 'more desirable'. There's a Chinese proverb that sums it up nicely: 'Love is giving. Desire is obtaining.' To be loved is to be truly known, good and bad, and to be deeply cared for within all those elements of your character. Individuals – their character, their quirks and intricacies, their insecurities, the things that make them laugh and tick and get them fired up: those things are as unique as your fingerprints (or indeed tongue print – which I just found out is different for everyone too). They can't be duplicated. They are one of a kind.

Be a person who actively looks to be attracted to those qualities. Push yourself to ask questions about who people really are – what gets them going, not what they can do to get you going. If you're really seeing people in this light, you'll see what there is to love about them, both romantically and platonically, far more easily.

DON'T let go of 'the red flags'

I've encouraged a certain liberality when it comes to deciding who to go on a date with, but there are some exceptions. There are red flags that serve as a clear signal to calmly move towards the nearest exit.

You don't want to date someone who judges. We're hard enough on ourselves without someone else chipping in and cutting us down on every decision, indiscretion or imperfection. If you're worried about something from your past, don't be. If it's in the past and you've got right with yourself and God, you don't need someone else to tell you it's OK. Because it is.

You don't want to date someone who doesn't treat people well. It's that classic thing where you're told to look at how someone speaks to the waiter rather than to you. If you find yourself with strong feelings for someone who is distant, unavailable or rude, then don't trust those feelings. The baseline for a relationship is that the person treats you and others with kindness and respect at all times. It is not acceptable or normal to deviate from that. Don't settle for anything less. A good test is to ask yourself if you would be comfortable being this person's ex. You may have to see them every week in church. You may have mutual friends. Your paths may cross from time to time. If the person isn't kind to others where there's a disagreement, or is likely to make things uncomfortable and unpleasant for you, don't go on a date in the first place. Dodge that bullet like you're Neo in *The Matrix*.

You don't want to date someone who is controlling. Initially, dating someone who is controlling can feel like less of a problem. At the beginning of a relationship, you're excited and you want to spend all your time with that person anyway. You're compliant. But that won't last, and if you have a partner who doesn't want you going out, spending time with friends and living your life, you're into dangerous territory. Don't complacently let your autonomy slip through your fingers. If you spot controlling tendencies, deal with it or get out.

You also don't want to date someone who wants to keep you a secret. If you can't be honest about a relationship, you probably shouldn't be in it.

Some of us have to reset what we see as 'normal'. If you believe that in every relationship the woman craves more of the man's time and is naggy and difficult, then that's what you'll settle for. If you believe that every man is distant and emotionally unavailable and would prefer to spend time with his mates than his partner, then that's what you'll settle for. What about a healthy combination of both people's preferences and expectations, all negotiated with a couple's good communication and some compromise? What if that's normal? What if relationships aren't stressful, anxiety-fuelled and lonely, but life-giving and affirming?

Bear in mind

If someone asks you out, it's not marriage – and you should seriously consider accepting. The only circumstance where I wouldn't is if I was absolutely certain it wouldn't go anywhere, and it would be cruel and tantamount to leading someone on to say yes. If you would enjoy two hours in that person's company, go on the date – attraction or not. You may surprise yourself.

When speaking to Foo Fighters about the circumstances under which they would ask a girl out, they were quite clear: 'Preferably, you would have spent time together as friends first, so you can be reasonably sure you want a relationship before you make a move.' While All Saints' attitude was: 'Christian guys don't want to ask you out because they think they're locked into a relationship if they do. It doesn't have to be that serious.'

Accepting a date from someone who is a question mark does not mean you'll miss 'the one'. You would never be afraid to go to a job interview for a role you weren't sure of in case the CEO of Google called and offered you an incredible opportunity. If the right person is coming, that won't be affected by this date. And this date could be the right person anyway.

At the end of the day, as Al Hsu points out, God sees far fewer wrong answers when it comes to dating than we do. Perhaps we should consider that he is more concerned with how we treat the person than who we choose?

A million ways to meet people

IRL

Meeting in real life has a number of obvious perks. You know far more quickly if you're interested in someone if you see the person standing in front of you. There's also the novelty factor. In a world where everyone starts their romantic story with a swipe right, you would still get to regale your friends with the story of a traditional meet-cute.

The best, most effective way to meet new people is to widen your friendship group. This means genuinely considering accepting every invitation sent your way, even if it involves dragging yourself out to a party or event when you'd rather be staying on the sofa. Once you're out and about, make an effort not to stick to the people you already know. Make sure the new faces see your face; and preferably hear your voice and engage in some interesting conversation with you.

Have you had a one-to-one conversation for a minimum of 15 minutes with each single person in your church? Not just the ones you think are fit. Every single one. When you meet people in real life, you need to be engaging with them for long enough that you can see why someone would find them attractive. That someone doesn't have to be you. But be interested in what they have to say and don't break away from that chat until you can list three attractive qualities about them. Your engagement will make them feel valued and, romance aside, it could be the start of new friendships.

The danger with asking someone out in real life is the added vulnerability that is not required when shielded behind a screen. If you know someone in person, you probably have mutual friends, or share a church or workspace or are at the same event. It means that if you get turned down, it's not just an unread dating app message, it's a face-to-face interaction and it could end in rejection. But bravery is liberating – I encourage you to try it.

Set-up

I've got a friend who is the last single bloke in his friendship group. He only dates 'by referral'. Experience has taught him who should (and should not) have access to the referral scheme. It is possible to get struck off. But with this system, he feels he is more likely to enjoy the dates that have come already endorsed by people he knows and cares about.

Great idea in theory, but setting two people up is, I believe, a matter of pure chance and not of any incredible insight (despite what that married woman from church who can 'claim five marriages' will tell you). People can have everything in common and not fancy each other, while others you would never have put together but they hit it off instantly.

Without fail, all the single people I interviewed for this book said they would like to be set up on more dates by their friends, but most had only had one or two set-ups and some had had none at all. I've set people up twice in my life. On the first occasion, I mutually agreed with a friend that we would each introduce the other to a date. I then looked through my phone and realized I had no idea who I could offer her. So, much like in *Friends* when Joey forgets to find a bloke for Phoebe, I started fumbling around in the dark. I remembered that a while ago I'd signed up to a Christian dating app for an article and had swapped numbers with a bloke. I had never met him; all I knew was that he was eligible. Sorry, not *eligible* – because I hadn't really had a conversation with him – he was fit. That's it, I meant fit. But so is she, so I thought fit + fit = great date. Can't argue with the maths. Except you can. It did not go well. He was distant and didn't make any effort with conversation. I had effectively condemned my friend to an awful evening with a good-looking but stand-offish guy. Much like recommending a book you've never read, this is a bad idea. There is an implied level of vetting in a set-up that it is polite to do. Only your mate should be going in blind.

The second time was far more successful. On this occasion I had met both parties plenty of times (my new baseline) and I knew that, at the least, they would enjoy each other's company. I asked them both if they would be happy to go in completely blind – no full names, no social media, not even a grainy WhatsApp picture to zoom in on. They agreed and so, in the most elaborate set-up known to man, I handled logistics, times, dates, meeting points and reservations; I even called up the bar and tried to have a cocktail waiting for them on arrival. It's fair to say I had upped my game since aforementioned blinddategate.

They met at Waterloo Station under the big clock – such a cliché but I'm not sorry. He refused to wear a red carnation, much to my chagrin. As a result, they had to settle for a description of the other's outfit as a tool for identification. Once they had met, they sent me a selfie and I replied with the instructions for the evening. These involved heading to a nearby board-game bar for an evening of food, drinks and Scrabble. They called it after three dates. But even if the love didn't, the legend of the spectacular set-up lives on.

If you can possibly do this for your friends, I would highly recommend it. Date administration kills the mood. If you can take logistics out of their hands, there's nothing to temper the excitement and anticipation. A couple of things to bear in mind before set-ups: some people love it. Some people are flattered and excited to meet a mutual friend. Others can find it awkward and uncomfortable and are bored with being sent off with any old person just because they happen to also be single and in the same age range. Check which of those camps a person is in before attempting an introduction. If one party is less likely to agree to the match than the other, start by clearing it with that person first. It would be tough for your friend to agree to a set-up that the other person rebuffs. You can establish if someone would be open to a set-up before you name the person you have in mind, just to protect the other party a little. But if someone does turn down your recommended date, communicate it with as much kindness as possible to the initial party and make it non-personal. 'They weren't up for being set up' isn't a lie, it's just not massively specific and that's OK.

Never set people up if they've expressed an interest in dating you. To them, it will feel like you're offering them a consolation prize. They don't need your pity or help with their love life.

Finally, stress to the two people that you think they'll end up great friends, to keep expectations low. Expectations are an even bigger killer of romance than date admin.

Arranged marriage

Seven of the people I interviewed specified that they were so fed up with dating, they would be comfortable with an arranged marriage. It wasn't in my set of questions. I didn't bring up the concept once. But people kept referring back to it.

Just to be clear, this is not a forced marriage, where two people are introduced and made to marry that instant. This is an arranged marriage, where the parents or families of the individual find a person they believe would be a good match, who fits in terms of age and faith, and make an introduction. There's no obligation to marry, but if the pair decide they are well suited, the expectation is that marriage will follow quickly. One Foo Fighter said: 'I wouldn't be opposed to the idea of bringing back arranged marriage at all. Provided the fundamentals were in place, I think I could make a marriage work with anyone.'

The more I explored the idea, the more it didn't sound crazy. The idea of knowing that that person isn't going to sweep you off your feet, but that love would be something you would build and grow actively became increasingly appealing. Zero romantic expectations, just a partnership to invest in. I was in. I called my mum. Here's how it went:

ME: Mum, I'm ready for an arranged marriage. I want you to ask around all your Christian mum friends and set me up with a nice boy.
MUM: Oh. Well, I'll have to think. What about Pauline's son, Ed?
ME: If Instagram's anything to go by, Ed's got a girlfriend, Mum.
MUM: Oh, yes, no I think you're right. Well, if David didn't have a girlfriend, he'd be a great match too.
ME: Yep, he's lovely. Anyone else, though, Mum?
MUM: I don't know anyone else, darling.
ME: That's all you've got to say on it?
MUM: Well, it is really. But I do think it's a good idea.

Brilliant.

One of the women I interviewed got further in the process than I did. After years of rejecting offers from elders in her church and aunties to make an introduction, she eventually relented and agreed to have a phone call with a 'nice man' who lived abroad, as recommended by an auntie. Instantly regretting the decision, she ignored a phone call, a WhatsApp call and a Viber call from the man in question. After a follow-up call from the persistent auntie, she did have a chat with the bloke, who spent 20 minutes 'mansplaining' the Bible to her. So she decided to leave it at that. The following week, the auntie arrived at her house to confront her and find out 'why she was not pursuing her blessing'.

Snowball sampling

In scientific research, 'snowball sampling' is where you identify a suitable candidate for your study and that person recruits future subjects from among their acquaintances. For our purposes, find someone in a genre of people you'd like to date and directly ask them if they have a colleague/sibling/equally-hipster-friend-with-a-nose-piercing to introduce you to. If you can't ask outright, make sure you're attentive to their invitations. Like attracts like, so it doesn't hurt to make an effort with their team.

A friend of mine took snowball sampling to the next level when she scoured the 'People you may know' section of Facebook and asked mutual friends for introductions to the eligible bachelors on the list. I'm not saying I necessarily recommend this as a course of action, but I think we should all take a moment to admire the resourcefulness.

Events

Aside from the standard places where people gather – church, weddings, parties – there are a number of specifically designed singles events tailored for purpose. Don't cringe. Stay with me. OK, no, you can cringe a little. Coordinated Christian fun can be nightmarish, but adding in a singles element could be peak tragic. However, it's not all Shloer and going round the circle to share the best and worst things about your day. Some of the events on offer are actually OK. The issue is that often the people you want to attend flat out refuse and those who are keen can form an unlikely motley crew. But maybe it's time to shelve your pride, gather up a group of friends and head to one of these to see what it's all about. Stop pretending to be above it. You're not fooling anyone.

Date my mate

The premise of this is simple: a guy and girl team up and go along to the event as friends, where they will then double date other pairs of friends in what is, theoretically, a less intense form of speed dating. I attended one of these events with a friend at Focus (a Christian festival) a few years back. The groups of attendees were clustered according to age: 18–26, 27–39 and 40+. At the time I was 29, so naturally wanted to date in the 27–39 bracket. The mate I brought, Angus, was 25 so naturally wanted to date in the lower age category. Angus won the heated conversation that was hurriedly whispered on the sidelines. As a result, at one point, I ended up on an actual date with an 18-year-old. Suffice to say, I did not find love.

Christian speed dating

In London at least, this exists, and I dragged two girlfriends to the basement of a B@1 in the West End to try it out. The concept is straightforward: women sit at tables and an equal number of men rotate, joining each woman for a brief date before moving on. My personal highlight was when one bloke asked my friend why everyone kept asking him where he went to church, not realizing he had signed up to a Christian evening. By the end of the night, everyone had dated everyone. We all filled in an online form and stated if we were keen to see someone again and, if they agreed, the speed-dating company swapped our details. This is a fast-track way to 'kiss a few frogs'. I'm not going to say it rendered beautiful results, but it was a fun variation on a classic night out. And I did end up going on one date afterwards so it can't be all bad. Warning: be prepared to put in the legwork to keep conversation moving. Interviews, however, have brought up less uplifting reports of speed-dating events where people who had registered never showed up, leaving a big imbalance in the sexes and a number of women to sit alone without a date for a fair portion of the evening. Moral of the story – if you've signed up, show up.

Dinners

There are a number of formats for a dinner designed for single people to meet. It can be as simple as getting a load of single people in a room and laying on some food. It can be a coordinated safari dinner, where three houses host and three groups move around and have a starter at one, main at another and dessert at another. Or even events along the lines of the ones my friend Ali arranges that I referenced in the Introduction – 'connecting Christians leading parallel lives'. However it's facilitated – or however you choose to facilitate it if you set one up – there is an art to the amount of coordination you include. Ali alternates men and women at the table but pulls numbers out of a hat to assign seating rather than taking it upon herself. She also poses an interesting question to the guests before they arrive so they have a conversation starter lined up for the dinner. And, as if that's not enough, if a pair decide to grab a drink after meeting at one of her evenings, she encourages them to send her the bill, so the first drink is on her. Genius, right? Disclaimer: no one has actually sent her a drinks bill; it would be a bit much when she's already cooked them dinner.

Holidays

Believe it or not, I've heard of a few trips planned where, while not advertised as such, the idea is very much to gather together a group of fun, unattached Christians for a week in the sun, on the slopes or shores. It's Christian *Love Island* without the weekly eliminations and overtly sexual challenges.

Two things to point out: this is pricey. There may be some who could afford to chip in for a camping holiday on the south coast, but only a small proportion who could splash out on a ski chalet (I don't ski but I've heard that, by the time you've got the gear and a ticket for the cable car lift thing, you've shelled out the cost of a down payment on a two-bed terrace in Hull).

The second is: this option requires a lot of admin. What you need is one really organized mate who relishes the chance to take on the Head of Ops role. Or maybe that's you? No one's embarrassed to invest time in finding a place to live or in getting a new job, so maybe there isn't a problem with investing that amount of time in coordinating a potentially love-life-advancing trip?

Online dating

You probably don't need me to tell you that this is one of the key ways people meet potential dates nowadays and, for this reason, 'online dating' warrants a couple of notes of its own.

Should you dating app?

One of the respondents to the Single Friendly Church survey in 2012 said the following of online dating: 'I feel for me that it would be giving up on God's plan and trying to make it happen for myself. I'd rather wait for his best.'

This is a problem I have on the Recovery Course. I can't tell you the number of times I've sat with someone who has said: 'I've prayed about this. I don't need to work a programme. I believe God will heal me and it will be miraculous.' I love the faith of these people but I don't see a lot of wisdom in this approach. I've never seen God zap addiction out of someone (although I believe he can and I'm sure it happens). What I have seen is faithful people using all the tools God has provided for them to achieve sobriety. It's slow and painful but when people invest in it the miracle always comes. I mean always. I can't say that if you invest in online dating your partner will always come. I have more faith in the Recovery Course than dating sites, I'm afraid. But I do know that sometimes God answers prayers with tools and opportunities you need to grasp and doing this isn't a betrayal of his best for you. You're doing it with him.

Thankfully, many people reading this will have already come to this conclusion and explored dating online. A lot of readers will be aware that the days when the internet was just an endless source of weirdos on Chatroulette are long gone. Now, you can meet some normal, even date-able, people – if you know where to look. If you're just opening yourself up to the idea of online dating, I hope this section will get you familiarized with some of the basics. If you've been dating online for quite some time, then take a big exhale. I hope this section will comfort you, entertain you and give you some new ideas for the dates ahead.

The bonus of dating online is that it opens up a world of opportunities for those on a search for love in 'thin markets'. And by that, I mean people whose dating pool is smaller, like those who are 70+, those who live in remote areas, those in gay and lesbian communities and people who are keen to stick within their religion. By choosing to only date other

Christians, you are narrowing your pool of potential mates. However, if you go somewhere where they are all gathered, you are far more likely to be successful. Enter: the internet.

A few things to note when deciding if you're going to online date. The first is that you will suddenly feel you have a lot of choice. Unfortunately for you, not every option is an actual option – that is, not every person you like the look of will match with you, and even fewer will engage in a conversation with you. There's also the risk that you may not get many hits, particularly if you're in a remote area. The sudden expanse of options can create in people 'shiny-thing syndrome', where they don't settle on one person because they always have their eye out for the next shiny thing; meaning they never fully invest in the person they're speaking to. You also run the risk of loading yourself up with dating admin. Maintaining profiles and continuing conversations with multiple matches is arduous. These days there are actual companies where the wealthy can outsource this task to flirtatious impersonators. And they say romance is dead . . .

You also need to bear in mind that, on dating apps, virtually every decision is made on visuals – it's a shallow environment. Some people aren't as kind as they should be. That doesn't mean that *you* shouldn't be kind. Remember that attached to every account is an actual person who lives and breathes and feels like you do. That person may be really excited to have connected with you. Round things off well; be honest and gentle with everyone.

Dating app forecast has potential to include: scatterings of people matching and then immediately unmatching; heavy instances of matching and then ignoring the person completely; potential for people to match because they like the look of your mate in the pictures and want an introduction; or the classic – matching just to ask for sex. Avoid responding to people who are affronted when you say you'd prefer not to continue the conversation. Be on the lookout for catfish. Stay safe, guys.

Which site or app?

If you've decided you can cope or continue to cope with all that (and more power to you), it's time to pick which app or site to go for. If you've only previously dated on one app, it may be that you want to explore diving into a different pool.

Match.com and eHarmony are designed for people serious about their quest for love and, while they are not specifically Christian, they offer opportunities to announce your faith and to meet people who share it. PlentyOfFish (or POF to its friends) also has this option but is anecdotally known to be a bit of a pick-up site – so use with caution.

Likewise, the secular dating apps, Hinge and Bumble, have an option to filter for faith. Happn and Tinder don't but you can choose to make this visible on your profile. Side note: as with all tech, it's a fast-moving world. By the time you read this, these apps could be well out of date. In which case, you'll need to do some of your own research.

The plus side of a secular app or site is that it is a wider pool and you are more likely to find people you are attracted to and want to date. But you sacrifice the certainty that they will have a real faith. Often you will find box-ticking Christians who were christened, or were raised by a Catholic mum and therefore consider themselves religious, but who don't attend a church or have a personal relationship with Jesus. But if nominal Christianity is good with you, this is the starting place. If you want more certainty that people are invested in their faith, you could try one of the specifically Christian sites out there, Christian Connection being the most well known, followed by Christian Mingle (which has fewer options, in the UK at least). These are like the Match.com of the church world.

If setting up a full-blown profile on a website isn't your bag, there are also specifically Christian dating apps. In the UK, the biggest of these is Salt (there is also Crosspaths, but when I tried it out it seemed to have a pretty small community, so slim pickings). Salt is often considered the Tinder of Christian dating, except with fewer 'Netflix and chill' invitations (praise be). There's a decent crop of people to choose from and you should be able to get a handful of good conversations going.

A word of caution: just because a person is on a Christian dating site does not mean they're dating with Christian principles. I just watched peak-trash dating show, *Too Hot To Handle* (2020), on Netflix (like *Love Island* but with less class – uh huh). When doing the introductions for each of the participants, one American bloke explained that he had just put himself on Christian Mingle to try to find a girlfriend. In his next breath, he added that women often complemented him on the size of his penis and it had been likened to a can of hairspray (I assume 400 ml rather than travel size).

On a more serious note, I have heard stories relayed of women feeling safer with men because they're Christian, only to realize that the men didn't have good intentions. I've also had one woman confide in me that she joined a Christian dating site, and the first profile she was offered was that of a man who had sexually assaulted her nine months previously. It breaks my heart to say it, but just because they say they're Christian doesn't mean they understand that no means no. It doesn't mean they will treat you well. These apps are great facilitators, but the algorithms can't filter out predators. Take all the same precautions you would if you were meeting any stranger. Stay in public, make sure someone knows where you are, leave the second you feel uncomfortable – even if you're worried it'll be socially awkward, rude or dramatic.

How to dating app

The profile

There is an art to dating apps and sadly (and in a very unchristian way), it is largely about aesthetics. In Aziz Ansari's research for his book, *Modern Romance* (2015), he found that 90 per cent of the decision-making process on dating apps is driven by pictures. I want to say a Christian dating site won't be like that. But I fear that would be a lie.

That doesn't mean we all dig out stock images of chiselled models and start catfishing people. It means we are aware that we want to give a good impression through our pictures. Best practice for photos: upload several (I've seen the Salt stats and people with six pics do far better than people with one). No weird-angle chin selfies or fuzzy/grainy pictures. There is also a real backlash against mirror and gym selfies. I think they're fine if they are a reflection of your personality. Anyone who follows me on Instagram knows I love a good mirror selfie – if that's the person I am, why hide it from a potential date? It's possible I will be sacrificing matches with people who are repulsed by them but I can't be everything to everyone. I agree – there's a wider question over whether I should be a mirror-selfie person at all, but that's one for me and my vicar's wife over a big pot of tea.

There is some actual research on what types of pictures are most successful (again, I got these from Aziz Ansari). Women were most successful with selfies with a slightly flirty, coquettish expression and a downwards camera angle. They were least successful with pictures of them drinking alcohol or posing with an animal. Conversely, men posing with animals were highly successful, as were muscle shots and photos of them looking away from the camera with a serious expression (think aftershave advert). Men, however, did not get a great response from pictures of them travelling, eating food or participating in an interesting hobby. You heard it here first, Rob – women don't give a _____ about your bungee jump in Bolivia.

97

One of All Saints had a picture withdrawn from a Christian dating site for inappropriate content. She was laughing, with one hand draped around a friend's shoulder and the other holding a glass of wine. She said: 'I don't know if it was the drinking or if they thought it was too much physical contact or if I was having too much fun. But they deemed it filth and shut me down.' Your guess is as good as mine.

Once you've got the pictures right, you need to give original answers to some of the questions on offer. Here are some answers that are not original. In fact, they've had so much mileage you probably couldn't flog them to WeBuyAnyCar.com.

Q: What does your faith mean to you?
A: Everything.

Q: I'm looking for . . .
A: Someone who doesn't take themselves too seriously.

Q: My pet peeve is . . .
A: Slow walkers/loud eaters.

Q: I'm overly competitive at . . .
A: Everything!

Q: The person I'd most like to have round at a dinner party is . . .
A: David Attenborough (could also be Louis Theroux).

Other tired statements include: 'I'm <insert height here> because apparently that's important', 'I have a XXX Uber rating' and 'Don't worry, the child in that pic isn't mine'. References to *Friends*, *The Office*, Pam and Mick from *Gavin and Stacey* and chat about how much you love dogs have all also been thoroughly worn out. Equally, don't try to start a debate about pineapple on pizza. Heard. It. All. Before.

So what should you write? Something individual that is a real reflection of you and the things you enjoy/believe/do/say in real life. There's no need to make it too intimate, but include things that allow for a conversational hook. Honourable mention goes to the bloke I found on Hinge who finished the statement: 'I found out recently . . .' with 'that all crisps go off on a Saturday'. Now that's the kind of A* content I'm looking for when perusing a dating app. Informative and funny. You can have that one on me if you like – if this book doesn't sell well, no one will even know you stole it.

If you're going on a secular dating site, my strong recommendation is that you don't just tick the Christian box and leave it there. I make a point of outlining how important my faith is on my actual profile so that people completely disinterested in Christianity know to stay away. I go for something like this.

Q: I want someone who . . .
A: Goes to church. My faith is really important to me and I would love to share it with someone. So hit me up if you put the 'stud' in 'Bible study'.

Big fans (Mum and Angus) will know that I've used that 'stud in Bible study' line in my writing before. When it's that good, it never gets old. Writing or rewriting a good profile takes a bit of time. Stick the kettle on, settle into the sofa, sift through your catalogue of photos and pull together some playful answers that are reflective of you. If you need a soundtrack to accompany this venture, I strongly recommend Whitesnake's 'Here I Go Again '87' (1987).

The algorithm

On dating apps, the algorithm is simple. You will get your best potential matches in the first few days. Therefore, don't be tempted to set up a 'holding profile' with just one photo and a few words about you, so you can peruse the types of people on there. This will mean your semi-effort is the one that will be viewed by the people who are the best potential match and you won't be showcasing yourself well at all. Launch yourself on the dating platform with your best foot forward. If you're nervous about what to write, ask friends who are on dating sites if you can play with their profiles for a bit so you can get a feel for the tone. Nothing wrong with market research.

If you stay on an app for weeks on end, you will start to get offered profiles that are less active: people who haven't logged in for a while or who forgot to take them down when they met someone. After a while, it's the occasional newbie and then the app graveyard. The lesson here is to go hard in the first week or so, because that's when you'll get the best options.

Beware of the algorithm, though; it is a far worse wingman than your mates. Once the sentimental software from Hinge decided to highlight a profile it thought 'I would really get on with'. It was my ex. I too, at one point, had thought we'd really get on. No one needs trolling like that when looking for love. The same Hinge algorithm once offered a friend of mine his own sister as a potential match, based on location and age bracket. Computers are smart, but they're not that smart.

The other unavoidable annoyance is the high probability that you will see people you know. This doesn't have to be awkward. If they're friends, I screen-grab the profile and send the picture to them with some side-eyes emojis and we have a laugh about our experiences on the app. If it's someone you know but not that well, either silently swipe no and move on or, if you're interested, swipe yes and see what the response is. Fortune favours the bold.

If you know you have a mutual friend with someone you see on an app and you fancy a date, I recommend messaging the mutual friend and asking to be set up directly. You don't apply for a job online when you know someone who works in the office.

The chat

First things first, and this goes for online dating or any of the aforementioned methods of meeting people: there's no point if you don't properly try. You may as well not bother at all if you're not going to put any effort into it. This means having real conversations. It means investing in each person and not opening up 30 chats. It means maintaining momentum with five conversations (maximum) so you give them a real chance. Don't be constantly wondering if you can upgrade. Just invest in the interactions you've started. The solution to dating in a small pool of people is to invest more thoroughly in each connection. To spend more time with each person you meet. My challenge to you is to make sure you have learned something about each person you talk to that you appreciate, before you take the decision to walk away. It's important to stop seeing the characteristics on people's profiles and take the time to see their character. It is people's unique personality traits that will cause you to fall for them.

Make an effort to find them. Dig deep if needed. If you don't explore who they are, you're just going to stand there admiring the aesthetics and that will only get you so far. The connection is in the conversation.

Also – and this is crucial – spend as little time as possible on messaging. If you've had a good back and forth and exchanged four or five messages, ask if they want to chat on the phone or to FaceTime. It doesn't have to be a date; it doesn't have to be serious. But you will waste time going round in circles with small talk if you don't step up your method of contact. The quicker you do it the better. The sooner you interact over the phone, the sooner you can set up an actual date or just (politely) write it off. It's win-win.

Finally, if you make it to an in-person date, give the person more time still. People get a bit weird on first dates and say dumb things. Sometimes they need space to relax in your company. Will van der Hart on The Dating Course suggests seven hours together should do the trick. That's about three dates. If you're unsure after the first and second, try again. If you're certain it's a no, then it may be kinder to call it.

Date adviser

Lauren Windle

★★★☆☆
££, British, European, Flexitarian

Ratings and reviews

By BenedictTheBaker
★☆☆☆☆ Reviewed 7 February 2020

Terrible value for money

I'd walked past Lauren a lot over the last few years in church but thought it would be a good time to make a booking. She was closed for January (No Man Jan) but had some availability in February. I was surprised by how busy she was but thought it was probably a good sign. Lauren chose the date: sushi dinner at Tooting Market followed by a Great British Bake-Off experience in a pub marquee. The location and ambience were great and the food was delicious but it just didn't represent good value for money. At the sushi bar, Lauren spotted a couple nearby eating from a huge platter and ordered the same, without checking the cost on the menu. This meant that when the bill came, I had to go and withdraw cash (after remortgaging my home and promising away my first child) in order to pay for it. Then at the baking experience, she showed no flair or passion for cooking but just spent the entire time eating lumps of icing from the 'decoration station'. Would not go back. Update: Lauren recognized the extortionate pricing and offered a 50 per cent refund, which I accepted.

By Leeroy476
★★★★☆ Reviewed 10 April 2019

Two dates too many?

I saw an ad for Lauren online but had already met her on a few occasions in person so decided to get in touch directly to make a booking. I organized a ping-pong table but had to book it for 4.30 p.m. as I'd waited too late to get a sensible time slot for a date. Lauren didn't seem to mind and still came dressed for going out-out, despite it being broad daylight just off the Old Street roundabout. Lauren quizzed me extensively about my faith and went as far as to recommend books I may find helpful on my journey. I endured further interrogation about my dating history, job and friends. She was also terrible at ping-pong. Despite the Spanish Inquisition, I attempted a second date, this time axe-throwing, which Lauren was significantly better at. After two reasonably enjoyable evenings, we decided to call it a day and commit to a friendship. I still book Lauren for walks, takeaways and the occasional 4 a.m. boxing-match viewing session, but these days they're mate-dates. I would recommend Lauren to those who are keen to have someone enthusiastically try to direct their lives for them.

By BarryClive
★★★☆☆ Reviewed 24 March 2018

Good if you can cope with tears

I thought I'd try out Lauren as she's on the floor below mine at work so really conveniently located. Overall a good experience. I went for the pre-date coffee option before committing to a full evening. After a positive experience, I decided to go ahead with a dinner. Lauren suggested a Valentine's meal that would be filmed, complete with interviews for her work as a journalist. Lauren often asked me to take part in articles and used anecdotes from our dates in her writing, the novelty of which wore off quickly. An upside was not having to travel for dates as we could just grab lunch in the

Itsu by the office if I had a spare half hour. Lauren was personable and friendly, and I would recommend her to others, although with some caution. When I called things off, we were in a busy Soho bar and, despite insisting quite forcibly that she was not crying, there were definite tears. Not advised for those who can't tolerate weepers.

Asking and being asked out: a user's guide

Should you ask?

I once ordered an extortionately expensive pair of tights online after being relentlessly presented with sponsored ads for them on social media. The overpriced hosiery was delivered in a plush sustainable-cardboard box, which also contained a bright green piece of card with the motivational quote: 'It's time to make your move'. Having had a bit of back and forth with a friendly bloke for the past few weeks, I took this as a sign from God that it was time to ask him out. Two days later (incidentally the same day my indestructible tights laddered), I dropped him a message.

He said he just thought of me as a friend and we have since built a really nice, completely platonic relationship.

There are a number of lessons here: (1) indestructible tights are not indestructible, they are a lie and a total waste of money; (2) not everything is a sign from God; (3) it's not the end of the world if someone turns you down.

If you don't know if you should ask someone out, you probably should. If you've liked that person for a while but feel any response to you is a bit ambiguous, you should probably just ask. It might not break your way, but at least you'll know. Scared of the rejection? You're stronger than you think: ask them out. Don't want to have to see them in church after? Switch to the morning service for a few weeks: ask them out. Worried it'll damage the friendship? It's not a straight-up friendship if you have these feelings anyway: ask them out. Waiting for him to ask because he's the man and you're the woman? Get on the right side of history, love: ask him out. I've asked out a handful of people, with varying degrees of success, but each time – rejection or not – I don't regret it. Because at least I knew either way.

At the end of every interview I did, I asked the question: 'If I was going to run a seminar for single Christian people straight after this, what would you want me to tell them?' Without fail, every single woman said we should be asking more people out. Some thought the men should be making more moves; others felt it was the responsibility of everyone. I side with the latter but you've got to make your own mind up. 'Shoot your shot', 'give things a go', 'just ask and see', 'be bold'. The message was loud and clear. Confidence is key; that's not confidence that they'll say yes but confidence that it doesn't matter if they say no.

How should you ask?

If you've decided to ask someone out, do it quickly. I've spent years gearing myself up to ask someone how he felt about me, and the time allowed for a lot of accumulated hope and expectation that was totally unnecessary. As I've got older, I've reduced the lead time down to a couple of days, predominantly for my own sanity. When asking someone out, be clear. Don't ask if they want to hang out, or go for coffee, or grab a drink. Use the word 'date'. Don't allow for ambiguity, even if you think it will protect your ego in the case of rejection.

There's no tried-and-tested way of messaging someone. Use the medium you usually contact them on. It doesn't have to be face-to-face or on the phone; it doesn't have to be with flowers or in some grand way. I prefer a cheeky voice note. If you do write something out, thoroughly check the spelling and grammar before sending. You'd kick yourself.

Keep it low-key but clear along the lines of: we get on well, I enjoy your company, I've considered the idea that we would be good together and would like to explore that with a date – if you're not up for it, don't worry at all, I thought it wouldn't hurt to ask. It's scary and vulnerable and the wait for a response is agonizing (see the note on 'Schrödinger's boyfriend' if you're worried I don't know what I'm talking about) but it's worth it.

Being brave is character-building and being vulnerable is the bravest thing of all. Every opportunity to open yourself up a little bit is an opportunity for growth.

Being asked out

Congratulations – someone is sufficiently attracted to you to want to spend a minimum of an hour and a half in your company, one-to-one. This is a big day. Whether you reciprocate those feelings or not, the first thing to do is feel flattered. It takes a lot to muster up the courage to ask someone out; it means putting feelings on the line and someone has decided to take that risk – for you.

Having read stories of my dating disasters and disappointments (more of this to come), you may have made the reasonable assumption that I'm not qualified to write a section on being asked out. Perhaps you think I should just stick to the Bridget-Jones-style weeping into a tub of Ben & Jerry's. Well, I'm going to take this moment, for my personal pride, to put it on record that, from time to time, and without any coercion, people ask me on dates.

When deciding on your response to date requests, don't overthink it. Don't ask yourself if you could marry them. Don't ask if they would be a good parent to your unborn children or if your sister would like them. If you would enjoy two hours in their company, go on the date. If you feel confident that, at the end of that date, you'll still only see the person as a friend, it's not out of order to kindly say that and give them the choice. Rephrase the following into your own unique voice: 'Gee, Benjamin(a), that is so kind of you to ask. I love your company and really value your friendship. I've only thought of you as a friend previously but would be happy to test the waters with a date and see if that changes.' Forewarned is forearmed.

Whatever your reply, think it through and be kind. If you know you're going to say no, don't make someone wait. For that matter, if you know you're going to say yes, don't make someone wait. It's not nice. As soon as you know your response, the other person should too. And that's not just me saying it, that's a Bible thing. When you have the thing someone is waiting for, don't make that person wait till tomorrow for it (heavily paraphrased Proverbs 3.28).

Next up, don't be weird or awkward about it. If you're keen, just say you'd love to and sort the logistics. You're not obliged to reciprocate, but you are obliged to make that conversation as comfortable as possible for the person who asked. Wording a rejection is really tough; just be kind and honest. Don't offer up a 'constructive' character assassination – just say you're flattered but not interested.

A few years ago, someone I worked with asked me out. He tracked me down on Facebook and sent a short but sweet message asking if he could take me to dinner. It didn't feel right for me so I turned him down. I can confidently say I did my best to follow the aforementioned guidelines and, at the time, felt quite pleased with how I had handled it.

A year later, three of us, myself, this colleague and a mutual friend, shared a cab home from a night out in Soho. He (a few beers deep) decided it was finally time to bring up the interaction we had neatly avoided discussing for the last 12 months. He recalled how he had nervously located my profile and sent the message. In my obliviousness, I hadn't considered that this would have been a nervous process for him at all. In my head, he had hit copy and paste on his standard greeting to new starters and as a result, I had ignored the message for a day or so. Unbeknown to me, the interim had been a period of nervously checking to see why I hadn't replied even though the message had been 'seen' almost instantly. He then read out the response I had sent him. My over-enthusiastic, peppy tone was poorly judged and I was at pains to stress how great – despite my not wanting to date him – he was. It was nauseatingly affirming. I also accused him of sending the message when drunk, as part of my break-the-tension 'banter', which was similarly poorly judged. The lesson here: you can be the person writing the book about dating and still make a right hash of it. With the best will in the world, you'll probably always get it a bit wrong. Do your best and send the non-patronizing, kind message you'd like to receive if you were getting turned down.

Schrödinger's boyfriend

Schrödinger's cat [shroh-ding-erz kat] *n. s.* **1** A cat imagined as being enclosed in a box with a radioactive source and a poison that will be released when the source (unpredictably) emits radiation, the cat being considered (according to quantum mechanics) to be simultaneously both dead and alive until the box is opened and the cat observed.

    Schrödinger's boyfriend [shroh-ding-erz boi-frend] *n. s.* **1** A man imagined as having received a message asking him out, who will release his response (unpredictably) at a time of his choosing, the man being considered (according to quantum mechanics) to be simultaneously both askee's boyfriend and not askee's boyfriend until the response is received.

26 December

Today I left one of my closest friends a 14-minute voice note explaining that I had caught feelings. After a year of hour-long phone calls, mate-dates at dusky restaurants and him cooking me dinners after long days at work, I had lost my head. We had in-jokes, always teamed up in board games; he told me I looked nice and we messaged daily. My head was gone and there was only one thing to do. Tell him.

    I braced myself for the rejection I knew was coming. I've developed mechanisms to cope with worst-case scenarios and I knew there was no way this one was going to break my way. I knew we were just friends. I knew he had no understanding of what this level of intimacy was going to cause. This was the first time I would ever confess feelings for someone knowing I would gain nothing. I knew I was sacrificing our friendship, but it was a fair trade for my sanity. I may love him but I love me more (credit: Samantha Jones, *Sex and the City: The Movie, 2008*). I had to get it off my chest so I could hear him unequivocally confirm that we were just friends and move on.

    With only minimal ad-libbing and the undesirable addition of a few tears, I delivered the carefully pre-scripted voice note. I explained how I felt and why that meant, for now, we couldn't continue our friendship. If we had been on reality TV, my vulnerability would have won me so many female fans, they would have been printing off my *Loose Women* contract before I'd pressed send.

Blue ticks after an hour. Agony. After two hours: 'Hey, I've listened to your voice note. I'm at the football now but can either leave you a voice note or call you tonight. Let me know which you would prefer.' Poker face. He's good.

'Dude, I don't know.' Nice one, Lauren – use an overtly matey term that'll detract from your declaration. 'Maybe drop me a line when you're free and I'll see if I am able/want to talk.' I will be both, but he doesn't need to know.

I round it off with: 'Sorry this is s*** timing.' Sorry I've pushed myself to the absolute limit with our interactions that you've had to spend the Boxing Day football with your brother-in-law, deciphering a weepy message from me. Sorry I couldn't hold it in. Sorry I don't actually care about the timing at all.

'No, no, don't apologize about that.' I could hear the sincerity in his tone as I read the message in my head. He's so great. *Head gone.*

At 8 p.m. we spoke on the phone. He acknowledged that in our inter-actions I did all the emotional heavy lifting and apologized. Then he said he needed time to think. *Think about what?* All I was asking was for him to leave me alone so I could get over it.

I asked what this time was for and he replied: 'I can't say in all honesty that we are just friends.'

With my lack of preparation for anything other than a blanket 'no', I then agreed to what, with hindsight, is the most ludicrous plan of action I have ever heard. He suggested we take some time to reflect and that January felt like a natural window for this. He said we could meet up in the first week of February to discuss everything. I, in my state of shock, said yes.

The parameters for the friendship hiatus were established; we agreed to both attend any group engagements we were invited to and not be weird, but all one-to-one communication is off the cards.

What I have just agreed to is effectively giving someone I've asked out 40 days and 40 nights to respond. He's been taking tips from either Jesus or Josh Hartnett. It's bad enough when someone doesn't reply to a message like that for a few hours or, worse still, overnight. But I have now signed up to an agonizing 40-day wait.

27 December

At first glance the idea of a break sounded good. Therapeutic. I could read another book or two. Practise the piano more. Work out for two hours a day. Really invest in self-care. But with a day to reflect, I've realized it was absolutely idiotic. While I don't know his answer, he is both my boyfriend and not my boyfriend. Right now, he's Schrödinger's boyfriend.

In reality, I am in a no man's land, where I will just be holding on till he has reached his verdict. I'm at *The X Factor*'s judges' houses waiting for Simon Cowell to call but his private jet needs a refuel. Of course, if this goes well and he decides to greet me at the beginning of February with a bunch of flowers and two Eurostar tickets to Disneyland Paris, all this anxiousness will pale into insignificance. What are 40 days when compared to a happy life together?

Experience has taught me that pain forgets, particularly when something positive follows. That's why women keep having children. But I just can't be that optimistic. I don't win things, I don't get what I want, I don't get the guy. This is more likely to be an agonizing extension of the anticipation of rejection. I am waiting for the sword to drop. Waiting for pain is often worse than the pain itself. But at least I have an end date, unlike poor Damocles.

28 December

Today at a family lunch, I thought I saw him walking down the street towards me. Unlikely as I don't think he spends a lot of time in Bicester. Then I accidentally called my cousin by his name. I can't get it out of my head. No matter what I'm doing or who I'm with, the waiting is looming over me. I remember one of the psychiatry lecturers on my Master's saying that your brain can only exist in a state of extreme emotion for 72 hours before the chemical levels will plateau and even out again. Surely that means this level of heightened anxiety is about to subside? Surely this is the worst of it?

29 December

I miss making jokes with him, so in lieu of speaking, I've read through all our old WhatsApp chat. My stomach is in a permanent knot. People walk past my house to the Co-op on the corner like my pain is irrelevant to them. The only ones to have taken note are the radio DJs, who are now exclusively playing music that is applicable to my life. I've run through every scenario, forcing myself to be reconciled to the idea of a negative outcome rather than get carried away by what ifs. The jury is out. He and his select group of confidants will no doubt be picking me apart now. My character, my looks, his connection with me. Am I good enough? Will they draw up a pros and cons list and tot up the totals? There's nothing I can do now. I've submitted my paper and I just have to wait. It's the not knowing that's the hardest.

30 December

I feel annoyed at him. He thinks we both wanted time to think. We didn't. I wanted time and space to get over him but how can I when I don't know what's in the box? He thinks he's being kind but this isn't breathing space. This is limbo.

31 December

I managed to sleep all of four and a half hours last night. I'm running on Instagram quotes and Brené Brown. I think I'm resigned to this background-level anxiety that will follow me for all of January. I'm starting to feel numb to it, comfortable even. At least with things as they are, I haven't lost him. He exists in all states in the box. We wished each other Happy New Year on Boxing Day but I still want him to send me a message; I want to know he's thinking about me. I hope this time shows him how much better his life is with me in it. My car broke down en route to my NYE destination. I was shaken and panicked as I waited on a grassy verge for the AA man for 45 minutes. It took all my willpower not to call him.

1 January

He's not going to message. He's not going to get drunk and not be able to resist. He's not a student in freshers' week. He's an adult. He has self-control. He may not even need to employ it to stop himself from calling me. I'm just going to have to wait it out. For another month. But what if this isn't just me waiting for a verdict from him? Do I want to date someone who clearly is so clueless as to the best way to act around people? Do I want to date someone younger than me and in no hurry to commit? But am I even *there* yet? If I were would it be with him? Would I be proud of him? Would he fit in with my friends? Does it matter? When all I want after a long day is to sit and talk about everything and nothing over dinner with him? What if the answer to all this is yes but his answer is no?

2 January

Brené Brown is no longer hitting the spot. I have progressed to power ballads: Whitney, Mariah and (crucially) Celine. Who knew S Club 7's 'Don't Stop' would be a comfort to both 13 and 31-year-old me? One week and the agony has subsided; uncertainty is my life now.

3 January

Today was a bit better. I discovered Joan and Jericha's podcast and wanted to tell him immediately. I went to the cinema this evening and turned my phone off for two hours. As I turned it on again my heart was in my mouth hoping he would have messaged. He hadn't. Maybe he's just done with me. Maybe it won't be 40 days. Maybe we'll just never speak again. I told two of my friends today over dinner that I'd finally confessed everything to him. They said I was brave. Maybe I am? I've done some daunting things. I told my mum I was a cocaine addict. I tracked down someone I went to school with on LinkedIn to apologize for bullying them after 12 years. I wrote about my story of addiction for millions of *Mail Online* readers. But this took more courage than any of that. I wouldn't take it back.

4 January

Today my friend gave me some bad news and I wanted to call *him*; I want him to be my person. The person I hide with. The person I run to. But I'm scared. I'm scared that I will get all of that and I will get hurt. That I won't be good enough. That I'm not thin enough, funny enough, pretty enough, feminine enough. Too bold, too brash, too loud. That I'm difficult to love. The only thing scarier than not getting him is getting him.

5 January

About once a day I decide it's time to call time on this whole thing. I'm done; hopefully he is too. But I always decide to just hold on for one more day . . .

6 January

I tell a friend what's been going on. She knows us both. She says it's exciting. Like a rom-com. Feels like there's a distinct lack of com if that's the case.

7 January

I don't know if this is worth it any more. I don't even know if I want this. I can't help but feel angry at the person inflicting this on me. I can't help but feel angry at God. It feels so unjust to be sitting here waiting like this. I run through scenarios where he's just living his best life, barely considering me. That he could have forgotten this whole thing and is just out there golfing or drinking with his mates. Or worse, on dates with girls.

8 January

I can't help but feel I'm the author of my own misery. Why didn't I just say no to the foolishly long gestation period and force his hand? I tell my friend Aaron who brings over ice-cream. He agrees that when you ask someone out and you're waiting for a response, every minute feels like two hours. I'm pleased he gets it but that doesn't stop me going through it.

9 January

Surprisingly peaceful day. Just enough on at work to keep me distracted. I had a therapy session, which majored on my present state of suspended reality. The therapist told me I wasn't contractually bound to keep to the

40 days; that if I felt ready, I could contact him for an update. I've lasted just 14 days out of 40. Yet further proof that I'm not Jesus. Another nail in the coffin for my megalomania. After two weeks, if he doesn't know, will he ever? I call it. I drop him a message and ask him if he can speak.

He can.

I call.

I open the box . . .

How *not* to first date (based on *actual* first date experiences)

- Forget date's name and use an entirely different one for two hours.

- Turn up with a homemade cake.

- Realize halfway through that you had a fling with date's identical twin in university.

- Ask date if they want a 'snoggy'.

- Turn up in crocs.

- Decide the date is going so well that you can really open up to this person and speak about your battle with porn addiction.

- Forget your wallet.

- Position your date with their back to the screen so you can watch the football.

- Call them 'dude' so much, they eventually shout at you because they don't want to be your dude.

- Spend the whole time explaining how 'crazy' your ex was.

- Faint.

- Have so many cocktails that you fall off your chair and then down some stairs on the way out.

- Go to the toilet every half hour and come back with an 'itchy' nose.

- Have gained three stone since your pictures but justify it by telling your date in detail about your weight loss plans this year.

- Fail to mention you're diabetic and then halfway through the date, take out a needle and stab it into yourself without explanation.

- Turn up late, order two shots of tequila, knock them both back in quick succession and then throw up down the side of the bar.

- Explain to your date how women 'only get worse' with age.

- Step in dog poo without realizing it on the way to a date, then tuck your leg up when you sit down only to have your date ask why there's poo on your bum as you get up to walk away.

- Tell your date about your love for the band A-ha! Explain how you follow them round the country and then bring their signed album out of your rucksack as proof.

- Get a text from your ex asking you to come over with a pregnancy test and spend the rest of the date debating whether it's acceptable to turn up with Asda own-brand or if you have to splash out on Clearblue.

How to first date

On occasion, unfortunate incidents are the fault of neither party and these are unavoidable. Take my mate 'Rose' and her date 'Jack'. Rose was standing in the Tube station waiting for Jack, who was a couple of minutes behind schedule. As she waited, a woman came over and said: 'He's not coming.' Bemused and uncertain of what was going on, Rose said: 'What?' At this point the woman broke character, laughed and said: 'Sorry, I'm only joking. But I'd love to tell you about our Lord and Saviour Jesus Christ.' Rose thanked the woman but explained she was already familiar with her Lord and Saviour. When Jack approached, he saw Rose standing with the evangelist, who insisted on leading the two of them through a salvation prayer (despite them both being confirmed Christians), followed by a five-minute blessing over the relationship before they headed off for their very low-key first date. Rose and Jack didn't have a second date. Moral of the story: sometimes you can do nothing weird but someone else will do it for you. You can't plan for it. But thankfully, there is a lot you can plan.

Logistics

If you're the one who's suggested the date, you should probably also have some idea of what you want to do. I strongly suggest that if it's a first date, you don't put too much effort in. People love elaborate dinners, thoughtful surprises or splash-out gifts once they already have an idea of their feelings. If they don't know they like you and you greet them with a mystery boat ride, candle-lit, three-course meal and a helicopter home, it will feel like too much too fast (and they may think you're a bit creepy). If that's your flex, save it for later down the line.

This is an opportunity for them to meet *you*, not the showcase of amazing dates you can plan. Go for dinner somewhere low-key or drinks at a pub. Coffee is also fine but can come across as a pre-date, like a dress rehearsal to establish if you want to see the show in full – the Foo Fighters guys call this 'date zero'.

Activity dates are great but can feel a little stale if you don't throw your all into them. Cinema is off the cards early doors, as you can't get to know someone sitting silently in the dark. Later down the line, the cinema can be a great date, particularly Everyman where you're on a sofa big enough for the two of you.

Don't rock up too late: five minutes is fine but keeping someone waiting for half an hour is a poor start. Also, you want to arrive relaxed and carefree, rather than bursting through the door with sweat dripping down your face and having to demand a glass of water and two minutes to catch your breath. If it's an evening plan, make sure it's actually evening rather than directly after work. There's nothing sexy about the corporate 'Thirsty Thursdays' crowd. Be sure you book a table for after that point when the restaurant has turned the lights from 'lunch' to 'flirty'. Finally, put your phone away and pay attention.

Conversation

I hate the idea of providing anyone with prescriptive rules about date conversation. What works for some doesn't work for others and it's really about judging the tone, mood and the individual sitting across from you. It's time to employ your emotional intelligence and common sense, but for those who have neither, here are a few things I think it's good to bear in mind.

1 Some people freak out on dates and lose the perspective they would usually have with friends. Stay calm, it's not an audition. It's just two people enjoying each other's company.
2 If this were a football match, you'd want to have about 50 per cent possession. Don't harp on about yourself. Don't hog the ball.
3 Ask questions related to your date and what that person has just said and then really listen to the answer. As one of the All Saints pointed out: 'Sometimes, as faith is the only thing that connects you, you end up down a deep theology rabbit hole. I don't want to spend an evening debating predestination. I just want to relax and get to know you.'

4 Don't tailor conversation so you can shoehorn in your own achievements. Don't ask if your date runs just so you can boast about your most recent ultra-marathon. There is nothing more attractive than an attribute you discover naturally later down the line.

5 Don't ask what the other person is looking for. What you mean when you say that is: 'Can I compare myself to your ideals?' It doesn't matter what your date is looking for; you are you. And if you really like someone, you run the risk of trying to adapt to the other person's checklist. This won't create a natural dating experience and your date will catch you out and realize you're not that person later down the line anyway.

6 Don't overshare. There's a time for your date to know about your faith journey, your past indiscretions and your exes. This isn't it. Keep it light, keep it fun; see if you can laugh together before you cry together.

Ultimately, I believe a date should be enjoyable, whether you're going to see the person again or not. It should be fun. At the Foo Fighters focus group, one of the guys stopped me to say: 'Lauren, you've used the word fun about 20 times this evening. My priority when dating isn't to have fun. It's to establish if there is compatibility and connection with someone quickly, so you can either progress it or cut it as soon as possible.' I laughed to myself the next week when one of the women in All Saints said: 'Sometimes it feels like a guy is ticking you off his list. Like he's systematically eliminating options. It can make a date feel like an interview process.' Yep. That makes sense.

Rounding off

Finishing a date well can be awkward. I often slip into conversation at the start of the date that I'm having a drink with a friend later, just so there is no expectation of allowing it to languish on into the early hours. If someone wants to call it after an hour or two, don't take it personally. Dates are intense. Some of us need to do it in bite-sized chunks.

A man doesn't have to pay on a date. If it's a pay-when-you-order thing, I suggest going in for rounds. On occasion I have paid fully for a date, including the time when the person 'left their wallet', but I always leave regretting it and feeling like I did so out of awkwardness. For me, going halves is the way forward. If you're a woman on a date with a man who really insists on paying, even after you've suggested half and half, then I say let him. But suggest you pay the next time. If you realize you don't want a next time, kindly explain and offer to transfer half the cost. Only fair. The only exception to the 'best to go Dutch' guideline is if the person has asked you out and then chosen somewhere massively expensive without checking budgets with you. That's all on them and their wallet.

Being tight won't get you a second date. Don't be like my date, Mojito Mick, who ordered a two-for-one cocktail at happy hour and asked the bartender to keep the second for him behind the bar, rather than offering me the complimentary beverage as a kind gesture (that would have cost him nothing). I know – I don't drink cocktails, but they could have done me an alcohol-free one.

Finally, a note on kissing. My opinion is that if you're both into it, there's nothing wrong with kissing on a first date. This is not based on science or biblical principles so take it or leave it. My nightmare scenario, however, is someone awkwardly diving in for a goodbye kiss just as my train's pulling in or (worse) with a waiting Uber driver serving as an audience of one. If you think you want to kiss, go for it in the body of the actual date. Don't tack it on the end. Kissing is fun; it allows you to see if there's a physical attraction and is harmless if administered properly and both parties are keen.

Disappointment

The immediate aftermath

Four hours ago, my boyfriend left my house having just broken up with me.

We'd been dating for just three months. The brevity of the relationship was probably a blessing, preventing me from gaining further momentum as I hurtled into it, but the duration doesn't feel proportionate to my level of investment. I treated every moment like it was contributing to something built to last. Those three months had thrown a number of trials into our collective path, and subsequently we were pushed into a committed, exclusive relationship quickly. We had to decide if we were all in or all out. I was all in. In three short months, we were introduced to friends and he had met my family. He became a part of my routine, a daily debrief I looked forward to before I went to bed. With hindsight I'll say it wasn't love. But in light of recent developments, the strength of my feelings is redundant. He explained to me today that he was not in love. And, crucially, didn't see any prospect of it.

When someone is in the process of breaking up with you, it's manageable. You can make a couple of jokes to ease the conversation. You can hug. You can laugh. You can cry if the mood takes you. It's all fine because the person is still there. You're doing it together. Even if it is breaking up, it's an activity for two with the only one in the world with whom you want to do activities for two. But the moment that person leaves, it's just you. You and the three-course meal you've lovingly prepared for the two of you to eat that night, sitting in the fridge. A tangible reminder of your over-investment in the relationship. Like spending the last three hours polishing the floors of the Titanic before it hit the iceberg. No one got to enjoy that shiny parquet.

And now I've got to unpick it all. The card games we played, movies we watched, food we shared, drives we went on, books we read, each of them a string stretching from me to him, connecting us; each requiring dislodging. Every cute in-joke and 'thing' we accumulated together is now just a series of memories that cannot be lobotomized; tools I will use for self-flagellation over the coming weeks.

I'm clawing around, trying to get some perspective. I want to helicopter myself out of my life to get a clearer view. I can't work out if this was worth it. If the fun we had and the intimacy we built was worth experiencing for the searing pain it's now replaced by. In time it won't hurt. It may even feel worth it. I'll tell friends I'm grateful that it didn't work out. That God really had a plan for me. But I don't feel that right now. Right now, if I could rewind and have turned down that first date I almost certainly would.

The pain is acute. It's physical. The lump in the back of my throat. The overwhelming feeling of tiredness coupled with the fear that I won't actually be able to sleep. Then fear for that moment when I wake up the next morning and remember what happened the day before. The weighty feeling dragging my stomach down towards my pelvis. It's *disappointment*.

I'm exhausted. I don't know if I'm sadder to lose him or to lose the opportunity to break free from dating. I don't want to go on another first date. I don't want to set up a dating profile. I don't want to laugh at some idiot's jokes. I don't want to feel someone out to see if we could be compatible. I want the last weekend we spent together. I want to sit under his arm and knit while we watch a film. I want him to look at me in the dress I put on specifically for him and tell me he's lucky to have me. I don't want anyone else to do that. I don't want to let anyone else in to do that.

So how do I plug this pain? As a recovering addict I've historically tried a number of things. Alcohol and drugs; even entertaining the idea creates an issue far greater than the one I'm currently facing. Although there's nothing like a break-up to remind you of the merits of black-out drinking. I could eat a lot – except I can't. In high-stress situations, the first thing to go is my appetite. I could call someone else I know would give me attention and affirmation. But all I would want is for that person to be him. I could call friends. Call my mum. Pray. Watch TV. Spend time with my niece and nephew. I could do all these things, but I don't want to do anything. There is nothing I want to do. Apart from check my phone for a message I explicitly told him not to send me.

My friends respond to my SOS with a battle cry of: 'You're amazing, don't change', 'You're wonderful, his loss', 'You know what you're worth though, don't you? He was lucky to ever have got the chance with you,' and 'Bastard.' I read all the messages several times. My sister reassures me it's nothing to do with me, just our connection. But isn't that worse? There's nothing I can change. There's no debrief or exit interview or feedback form with action points. There is nothing I can do to protect myself from having this happen again.

Where was God? This omnipotent, omnipresent, all-knowing, all-seeing Father. Couldn't he have given me the heads up? Couldn't he have cut it before it even started? Couldn't he have saved me this pain? They say Jesus experienced every range of human emotion. They say he knows how we feel. But does he? Did anyone ever dump the Son of Man? I know the drill. I'm supposed to turn to God. Cast my burdens on to him. I know he's there, but I can't feel his arms around me. I know he loves me, but I don't feel it right now.

Sinking in

Filling every moment feels like an arduous task. I can't even contemplate what I've lost and the regret I feel at some of my decisions. How can I write a book about dating when, in this moment, I truly believe the only way I will fully get over this disappointment is if I meet someone else I like more? When I'm secretly planning a PG-13, Christian equivalent of 'get over them by getting under someone else'? Not through God, but through another relationship. How can I write a chapter about dealing healthily with disappointment when I have already internally committed to losing a stone in response?

I've tried praying. I don't know if I'm doing it because I feel it or because I know it's what I 'should' do. I know it's what other people would tell me to do. I've encouraged countless people in their darkest moments to just ask God to step in and I truly believe he will and does. But that's what I believe for them. I don't even know if he's hearing me right now.

I feel tired by the prospect of every part of my future. When we were together, I could envisage myself slotting into his life. He had a vision for what God was calling him to. I was ready to ride on his coat tails and make his plans mine. Making decisions for yourself with no collaboration is tiring. I'm ready for someone with decent judgement and a kind heart to come and take over. I want to use the pronoun 'we' and when I'm too tired to form my own opinions, I want to default to his. Am I putting too much pressure on him? Is that why he left?

I'm scared that my failed relationships and inability to find someone to share my life with will mar every positive experience I have. That I will never fully enjoy anything because in the back of my mind I will always know that I am alone. I am no person's priority. And I could end my life having always been single and wasted time feeling the pain of unsuccessful relationships. I'm scared that it will be the undercurrent of my entire existence. That I will waste my life feeling this recurring disappointment.

Post-mortem

We spoke on the phone today and I loved speaking to him. When I got off the phone, I had to remind myself we were discussing logistics for a break-up, not a first date. I play out full-length fantasy scenes where he's dramatically changed his mind. I wonder if I have a big enough vase for the excessively large bunch of apology flowers. One friend told me about a couple where the guy 'had a wobble' and broke up with a girl, only to realize his mistake and they're now married with a baby. But I drag myself back to reality by reminding myself of the headline: 'He doesn't love me and he never will'. Harsh but helpful.

We made plans to exchange items lent or left at the other's house and he suggested there may be things we didn't think to say in the emotionally charged, initial conversation, which we may want to bring up over a coffee. Presumably for the sake of closure. Instead, I feel like I'm about to conduct a post-mortem on a body that is still breathing. The build-up to the meet-up is always horrific. You know it's going to hurt but you can't plan or prepare yourself because you don't know how much; it's as if you know someone's going to punch you in the face but you don't know if they'll skim your cheek or spark you out.

As the week crawled on, I accumulated notes on my phone. Every angry, regretful thought. Everything he should know or should have done. Every rumination that had a right to be expressed. Every time

Disappointment

I beautifully articulated something to a friend noted down so as to capture the perfect phrasing for the confrontation. I tracked when the dreaded meeting was less than 24 hours away, keeping a mental note of where I would be at that time the following day. I forced myself to stop preparing for each eventuality. I forced myself to banish every positive thought about the interaction. I took everything captive and made it obedient to Christ. Jesus is currently holding my entire thought catalogue in custody.

The morning of the meet-up came with nervous energy and dread. I prayed. I wanted it to go away. I asked, at the least, not to leave with more pain than I started with. I deleted the list of notes I'd been adding to over the last seven days without rereading it. I prayed that God would help me to respond in the moment. No built-up, witty observations or attempting to mould the conversation to my agenda. He'll read this eventually anyway, so there's no danger he'll miss how this time has been for me.

I drive to his house. Loud music, I scream-sing along; anxious but with an eerie sense of peace. He's there: the focus of the entirety of my mental energy for the last eight days, standing in front of me in unwashed shorts and a T-shirt. Close enough to touch. But I don't. We get coffee and food and sit in the park. I barely eat; I don't even have the capacity to pretend I'm eating properly. We talk. I miss him. I want to do this debrief every day, accepting the scraps of relationship on offer. I want him in my routine.

None of his doubt from the previous week is still there. I prayed that he would be certain. When I'm picking between two chocolate bars, I'll do an ip-dip and the moment my finger lands on the Kit-Kat Chunky, I realize I wanted the Kinder Bueno all along. I thought this might be the same; that settling on a firm choice would allow him to see what he really wanted. It looks like it did, but that just wasn't me.

We sit for hours talking. He catches me up on all his friends. A final instalment in the journeys I've avidly followed. The mailing list I'm now unwillingly unsubscribed from. We discuss what kind of friendship we'll be left with. I don't know what I'll be able to muster in the future, but for now I offer him nothing. I ask how he'd feel if he had to be around me with someone new. He said he wouldn't mind. He's so sure that he only wants a friendship with me, that seeing me move on would cause him no pain. That's when the punch in the face landed.

I'm sitting with him, but I feel alone with the excruciating realization that he doesn't feel what I feel. I feel angry that, since the day we broke up, he hasn't expressed any sadness, any doubt, any disappointment. I feel left behind. Still sitting in a room he walked out of a long time ago. The one-sidedness feels unjust.

I'm annoyed at myself for the strength of my unreciprocated feelings. I'm annoyed I didn't take the chance to be angry earlier on. I want to take back every long conversation with my friends, every day I spent feeling sad, every time I cried. He wasn't doing the same. I can see that conversation is winding down, so I call it before he does. I want to stay, to soak in every second he'll stay with me but what would be the point? I can't let him see how hurt I feel.

He walks me to the car. We hug but I don't hold it long. I don't want to. I have to get out. As I drive away, I turn the music up so loud I can't think. I don't allow my mind to budge an inch from the emotional tightrope I'm balanced on. I just have to get home.

There are times when I love solitude but now it feels oppressive. Suffocating. Like banishment for those who can't make a relationship work. My empty house stands like a relic of our time together. A mausoleum. Every corner a memory, a tool for torment. Having forgone the opportunity to pick apart every crevice of our relationship with him, I'm left to make my own assumptions. I'm battling my own head and urging myself to leave it alone. *When did he stop wanting to move forward with me? When did he know he would never love me? Did I say something? Did I do something?* I mentally run through every time he laid foundations, he pushed things forward, he pulled me closer, just to reassure myself I wasn't crazy. But none of that matters now. Every plan we made is a broken promise. At first I prayed that he would change his mind. Then I prayed that one of us would. Now I'm just praying that I will. And quickly.

Glimpses of calm

It's well past the immediate aftermath but my friends persist in supporting me. I've had messages from people first thing in the morning, acknowledging it's a tough time of day, numerous bunches of flowers and cards. Tessa even sent me a lavender pillow spray to help me sleep. Rachel sent me a to-do list: *Go on a walk/do gentle exercise of some sort, eat little but often, drink lots of water, open the Bible at least twice and sit in the Psalms, find a verse you're going to chew on all day that brings hope, call a great friend* . . . I'm calling this Plan B. Plan A is not eating, praying, washing or getting out of bed, and binge-watching episodes of *Ex On The Beach*. It's hard to know who's got the better strategy.

I'm now getting served ads on Instagram for life-coaching apps that show you how to 'get over your ex' and digital clairvoyants who, for a small fee, can tell me 'if he's still thinking about me'. As if a break-up isn't bad enough, now I've got the anxiety of knowing the machines are listening to my every word. Still, I'm starting to feel better.

The acute sting is gone. Now I just feel bruised. The world feels a bit sadder. I don't want to keep wishing away moments and counting down time in anticipation of when the ache will lift. I'm ready to feel normal again but it's just out of reach. I want to believe Clare when she says it'll pass. I'm bored with Bible verses about comfort and 'seasons' and hope. Realistically, I recognize this will pass. It's not my first rodeo. Ten years ago, almost to the day, I lost the man I thought was the love of my life. I thought the world had stopped. I thought every day I lived would be worse because he wasn't living it beside me. But as time went on, I realized I was nothing but grateful. I can't imagine the different, less fulfilled, drink-and-drug-fuelled life I would still be enduring if he hadn't walked away. I thank God for every step he took back to his car after he dropped me at my mum's house.

When my parents retired and moved to Devon, they viewed houses all around the south. Ideally, they wanted a sea view. But the cost of having an unobstructed view of the coast was often prohibitive so they found themselves looking round a number of properties with what estate agents optimistically described as, 'sea glimpses'. A sea glimpse is where, if you pull a chair up to the back-bathroom window, crane your head to the left and slightly squint with one eye, you can convince yourself that the patch of blue is in fact the sea. I've progressed to sea glimpses. Every now and again I feel a sense of calm. I don't know if I'm actually seeing it, or so desperate for it that I'm being duped by a mirage. But I get the feeling I might be OK.

Tonight, I prayed again. This time I didn't just reel off the things I was supposed to say. I didn't just put on a brave face and tell God I knew he would make it all fine. I got on my knees and prayed a prayer of lament. I asked God where he was. I told him how I was angry and upset. I needed him. And I stayed there. This time I asked him to come and sit with me where I was instead of asking him to take me out of it. I felt raw and bruised and heartbroken. But for the first time, I didn't feel alone.

Closure

I'm done. I'm done living in my tracksuit and not drawing the curtains. I'm done responding to my friends when they ask how I'm doing by just saying, 'Badly'. I'm done checking my phone for messages he's not going to send. I'm done running through fantasies where we both happen to be in the same karaoke bar and I (post-aforementioned weight loss and a blow dry) get up on stage and sing Toni Braxton's 'He Wasn't Man Enough For Me' without dropping a note. I'm done wondering if he's wondering about me. I'm done wondering if he regrets it. I'm ready to move on.

With a bit of time, I can see that, despite the strength of my feelings, the relationship was fundamentally flawed. We both made mistakes. I don't know if I want him back but I do know I don't want the relationship back. I don't want the uncertainty of the last couple of weeks and the unresponsiveness and distance I've felt. I don't want someone who takes every opportunity to pull back from me. I don't want to feel so insecure that I bend over backwards to perform to keep someone interested. I don't want to cook three-course meals. I don't want to plan outfits. I don't want to google date ideas weeks in advance. I just want a break. I just want to feel certain and comfortable. I want to delight in the mundanity of security. I want someone who feels like home. But my responses towards him were on me. He never asked for fine dining and rabid attention. Those are my lessons to learn.

I've had to force my thinking away from what he would think of this outfit, this trip, this decision and ask myself what I think. As an individual. I recognize that I should never have been incorporating his preferences in my decision-making process at this early stage anyway. I've come to terms with the idea of giving up the plans and hopes and dreams with him. I'll still achieve and enjoy those things, whether on my own, with friends or with a future partner.

In time I'll work through the fear, a fear that long outdates him. The fear that I'll have to experience this pain again. The fear that I will meet the love of my life, but I won't be his.

The Bible tells me to rejoice in trials (James 1.2). Instagram tells me that 'straight roads don't make skilful drivers'. I can see lessons. I've journaled them and prayed about them.

Here's what I wouldn't have been able to hear when I first sat down to write this chapter: God has been there. Not in the immediate quick-fix way that would have been my ideal, but slowly working away, clearing a path through each day for me. I don't know how people do this without God. Maybe Jesus was never dumped, but the rejection he experienced was unparalleled and far beyond my understanding. It was public and brutal and undeserved. It goes without saying, I wouldn't swap.

On reflection, this experience will make me stronger. I just pray I'm done now. I can't handle more growing pains. I don't know what I'm left with on the other side of this, but I don't need to know right now. My only job is to do today well. Be proud of my decisions and keep God close. To me, exes are like alcohol. We had some good times; we had some bad times that ended in me feeling a lot of pain. If I turn up at a party and it's there, it's fine. It doesn't affect my enjoyment of the evening just because other people have brought it along.

But I don't want to take it home with me again.

Calling it a day

In the immortal words of Björn Ulvaeus (1976), breaking up is never easy (I know). Often the people who do the dumping are vilified and others assume they've escaped unscathed, but the fact is, no one wins in a break-up. It is true that the ones administering the break-up have known about it longer and had more opportunity to come to terms with it than the other parties. Therefore, it's possible they will move on more quickly. Plus they have the added bonus of it being their choice. But there's pain to be experienced on both sides of the battle lines. No one can tell you when it's time to walk away from a relationship. There's no checklist or set of instructions. The only advice I can offer is that doubts are normal and shouldn't be fatal. But when you've moved beyond doubt to a place where you know there's no chance of progression, the kindest thing is to cut it off.

Disembarking from short haul

If we're talking not-really-feeling-it-after-one-or-two-dates vibes then there is sometimes a temptation to gradually be more distant on messaging, until you stop replying altogether and claim that things 'just fizzled'. This is called ghosting. It's a hard no. No matter how casual or nondescript your dates were, you need to send a rounding-off message saying that you're not interested in a second/third/future date. It doesn't have to be big or dramatic. And if the person replies saying, 'Thanks so much, I was thinking the same thing', just let it go. They may even be telling the truth.

Disembarking from long haul

If you're not sure if you're short or long haul, assume you're long. It's better to treat the relationship with more respect than it warranted than misjudge the situation and go for less. For longer-term dating or relationships, breaking up should be done in person. If, for some reason, geography or an act of God or a pandemic (*coughs*) prevents this, then make every effort to make it as personal as possible – over FaceTime or a phone call. Never text or email.

The key is open and honest communication in the run-up. If you've expressed some concerns then it won't feel like you've gone from 100 to 0 when you finally call it a day. Sometimes, it can be helpful to involve the other person in your thought process to avoid a big shock. You don't have to put on an 'everything's normal' face until you drop the bomb. There doesn't need to be a big reveal. It's not a surprise party.

When you do sit down to have the conversation, your priority is being kind. Bear in mind that less is more. Don't fill every second of silence. Don't just keep talking. Pray about what is wise to share and restrict yourself to that alone. If you know it's a break-up and not just a discussion about your relationship, use those words early on. Say: 'I think it's best we break up.' Don't let the other person spend half an hour trying to groom the horse without realizing it's already bolted. Say something great about your soon-to-be ex but don't wax lyrical about it. Don't overdo it. You'll just _____ the other person off. If you really thought this was the most exceptional person you'd ever met and whoever your ex-to-be ends up with is really lucky, then you wouldn't be finishing it and that lucky person would be you. Stick to the truth, without hyperbole.

Next, explain why you think it's not working. Not why the other person isn't working but why the two of you together isn't working. That your connection isn't right. It's OK to say you're not feeling as attracted as you had hoped, but it's not OK to explain that that's because the more you look at the person's nose, the more it seems to be taking over their face. No personal or potentially hurtful comments.

I feel strongly that, in a lot of cases, it's not helpful to tell people exactly why you don't want to date them. This contradicts a lot of other dating books that suggest giving people feedback they can build on. Before you assume the role of their life coach, I think you've got to ask yourself if you're the person best placed to help with their character development? Are you sufficiently objective? Do you have the right to speak into their life like that when you're dumping them? To my mind, you're about to do enough damage. You should probably keep your opinions to yourself.

When giving a reason for breaking up, don't say it if it's not true. If you say, 'I've got a big project on at work and I don't have time for a partner', the person will be waiting for you to come back when the project is over. And you won't. Because the project was never the issue. And then your ex will feel rejected and lied to instead of just rejected. Or worse, an ex will see you on a dating app, know the project isn't over and then will realize – along with everyone else they know – that you're just an idiot.

Avoid clichés: 'it's not you, it's me'; 'I need time to work on myself'. Lazy. And never blame God. Don't tell someone you don't think God wants the two of you to be together when you just don't fancy that person. Don't give anyone a reason to resent God. That's not fair.

It's so important to be kind in your explanation. Think about how you can leave people better off than when you found them. How you can uplift and encourage them. Not leave them with more insecurities and scars than they started with.

Next up, you've got to give them space to respond. This is something Sheila from the previous note did very well. (I didn't name him because he chose the pseudonym Sheila and the ridiculous moniker would have really messed with the tone of the piece.) He gave space for response during the initial conversation but also suggested a catch-up a week later when the dust had settled, to allow for anything that had been ruminating to be expressed. Well played.

The key to breaking up well is not to leave any shades of grey or glimmers of hope. Don't say anything that will give people the impression you will change your mind. As tough as it is not to sugar the blow, they need to know what they're working with so they can start to move on. Once you've clearly expressed yourself and they've had the chance to respond, you should leave. They need to deal with the aftermath of this away from you. They have friends. It's not your job any more. From now on, they will have to cope with every upsetting situation they come across without leaning on you. That starts now. Brutal but important.

And finally, never break up with someone when you don't mean it. Never end things to scare someone into changing or to make a point. Don't walk out of a room expecting someone to chase you. Attention-seeking is ugly and transparent and cruel. The other person may call your bluff and your attempted manipulation will render you alone.

Being broken up with

Being broken up with is _____. Job number one is to get through the actual breaking-up part with dignity and then you can deal with the inevitable emotions afterwards. When someone breaks up with you, hear that person out. Stay silent as much as possible and let them talk, explain, fill the silent void with words. A friend once told me you can discuss and debate and argue with the police all you like, but the minute you hear them read you your rights, you shut up and let it happen – that is, the second you are under arrest it's time to comply. If I'm honest, I think we should probably all just be polite and comply with the police whether we're arrested or not, but I do think this analogy applies in break-ups. You can debate and negotiate and discuss as much as you like, but when one party has made the decision, don't fight it. Let that person walk out of your life. If you're holding out hope for a comeback, that's far more likely if you've conducted yourself with grace.

If you have questions, you're entitled to ask them. But I would strongly advise that you think through how much you need to know. Will the answer be helpful or painful? What will it change? Why do you want to know? Resist the urge to ask what it was about you the other person didn't like or love or wasn't attracted to. Often people can't put it into words; it just didn't click. But if they do have a reason, hearing it gives their opinion far too much power. What they think of you is irrelevant now. What matters is what you think of you. If you're concerned you need some self-development, ask a friend who knows you well or give someone who loves you the invitation to speak into your life or ask God. Don't ask the person who has just hurt you – your investment in the answer will be so tied to your current heightened emotions, you will give it too much weight. You haven't been interviewing for the role of partner and have just been fired after the trial period. This isn't about the other person's assessment of you. If it's something you can change, you may try to, whether that's right or wrong. If it's something you can't change, you may obsess over it. It may become the focus of your mental energy; you may start to become self-conscious about it. It may affect your self-esteem. It's like when your computer can't connect to wifi and suggests you run diagnostics. You can run diagnostics if you want but the response that comes back is often vague and difficult to understand.

It doesn't fix the problem, nor does it offer any insight. Save yourself some time.

When someone breaks up with you, it is not your time to offer a rebuttal. A break-up is the best time to show someone you understand your worth. Don't plead, don't beg, be polite and then take your anger and pain somewhere else. Lines like: 'You're looking for something that doesn't exist' and 'You'll never find someone else like me' are pointless. That person doesn't want someone like you, otherwise why break up with you? And if someone doesn't know what they want that's on them and God. If they die alone after rejecting a string of amazing partners, it's not your problem.

What next?

I do think in a lot of cases it's helpful to schedule in a chat about a week later, in person or over the phone. It provides space to discuss anything that didn't come up in the initial conversation after a bit of processing. This is also a good time to deal with the division of assets – for you to return T-shirts or books or the vintage 'GameBoy with Zelda' game you borrowed. But don't drag it out; don't call or make contact unless strictly necessary. Never drunk dial. If you can't restrain yourself, delete their number. Once the admin is done, as hard as it is, cut all contact. You will get over this so much more quickly if you do it without the other person. Don't put things on social media in the hope your ex will see them; don't run through your stories to see if they've viewed them. Mute your ex's accounts so you don't have to see what's going on. If you do keep their number, change the name in your phone from nickname/first name to full name. The name you used before will be highly linked to dopamine release for you. Change it so you don't get that jolt of stimulating hormone when it pops up any more.

When people say they don't see a future with you, it's important to take them seriously. Pining for them and hoping they will come back is an expectation that is setting you up for disappointment. Never chase love and affection that isn't freely given. Don't reach out to someone who isn't reaching back. You're worth so much more.

Your only job now is to take time to heal following this relationship. To grieve the loss of that individual. To grieve the loss of that level of companionship and to grieve the loss of the future you had hoped for together. Pray when you can and what you can. Explore lament and try to put it into practice when you're ready. You can be a modern-day psalmist. It may feel self-indulgent and wallowy but it's real and it's how you feel. Allow yourself to feel pain. This feels like a passive act, like you're not doing anything. But you are. It's brave. Sometimes feeling it can become claustrophobic. Don't allow yourself to get trapped by it. Open a window and do something for yourself to let some air in. You won't enjoy it but it's good for you. You can build something around your hurt that's positive and helps you cope. Interact with the sadness, go for a walk, take it with you, have a hot chocolate.

Take it from a recovering drug addict, numbing it out doesn't work. Cutting someone off you thought would be in your life for ever is like going cold turkey. You can suffer withdrawal. But you will get through it. Don't berate yourself for how long it takes you to get over someone. There's no formula. It doesn't really take a third of the length of a relationship to move on. It takes as long as it takes. But don't grieve like someone who has no hope (1 Thessalonians 4.13) even though, sometimes, hope can be the most painful thing of all.

A word to the broken-hearted

Every time I hit a romantic disappointment, my friend Tessa sends me the same video clip on Instagram (I'm embarrassed to see how many times it's popped up in our messages). It's an American woman saying: 'You're a catch, act like one' (makerswomen, 2019). You really are. You want to date someone who thinks you're too important to lose. But sometimes the relationship just doesn't work for one or both parties. What would it mean if everyone could develop this amazing connection? It would make the world straightforward and everyone interchangeable. The varying interactions you have and the depth you can reach with another person are part of the beauty of life. It's horrific when your feelings aren't matched. But experiencing it will make you stronger.

I want to sit with you. I want to bring some industrial-strength glue and see if we can stick your heart back together. I want to cry with you. By reading this book, that's what you've done for me. I'm sorry I can't do that. But I pray you have friends who will sit with you and do nothing;

who will let you cry without trying to fix it. And in lieu of my company, I've made you a gift: three playlists for the broken-hearted. Wallow, seethe and eventually move on with every song I blasted when I felt low. They're on my Spotify – <https://open.spotify.com/user/1180141640> – and I made them, with a little help from my dad, specifically for you.

The exception that proves the rule

It's a familiar scenario: we're stuck in a situation and things aren't going our way. But as a consolation, we drag up from the back crevices of our mind a story we're pretty sure someone once told us, where the subjects had a miraculous, happy ending.

This unlikely yarn brings us new hope because, if it happened for them, it can happen for us. The brutal reality is, it can happen for us, but it won't. Often these dramatic and fortuitous stories are complete one-offs. And rather than serving as a model for us, their uniqueness – demonstrated by the fact they made it through the grapevine to you – only further confirms the existence of the pattern. These stories do happen. But they wouldn't be miraculous if they happened to everyone. So they're unlikely to happen to you. If one of the fables below sounds all too familiar, it may be time to tell yourself a new story.

The friend and the revelation

Once upon a time, your mate from home group's mate Robbie had been pining after a friend for a number of years. Waiting in the wings with fingers crossed, Robbie hoped this friend would suddenly realize what a great team they were and would make a move. One day, Robbie prayed that the person's eyes would be opened to him as a future partner, and this friend suddenly saw him in a whole new light. The two of them fell in love and lived happily ever after.

The idiot and the turnaround

Once upon a time, someone from CU at uni told you about this person called Emma, who was in an unhappy relationship. Emma loved her partner but struggled as this was someone who could be difficult, demanding and unreasonable. She decided to stick it out to see if things would change. In time the partner grew and completely transformed, seeing the error of those controlling and volatile behaviours, and the relationship settled into a life-giving, fruitful one. And they lived happily ever after.

The break-up and the change of heart

Once upon a time, this person named Ross, who you think you bumped into at a festival three years ago (but that could have been someone else) was in a relationship with someone but got the jitters. Terrified of the looming beast 'commitment', Ross called the whole thing off. But after a couple of weeks, he realized he had made a terrible mistake. So he retraced his steps, confessed the error to his heartbroken ex, who in time forgave him – and they lived happily ever after.

The non-Christian and the conversion

Once upon a time, this person at church's colleague's sister's friend, Alex, started dating someone outside church, who she fell madly in love with. Aware this was not the ideal scenario for her faith, but convinced of the strength of her feelings, Alex was tormented. She started praying day and night for a miraculous conversion. One day, after expressing an interest in hearing more about church and then going on an Alpha course, her partner became a Christian, the pair got married and they lived happily ever after.

The surfer and the miraculous message

Once upon a time, Aaron was coming out of the water after a long session on the beach. As he emerged from the sea, he locked eyes with someone walking in the opposite direction. In that instant, God said, 'That is the person you will marry.' Unsure if he heard right, Aaron asked God again and felt sure he got the same response. So, he ran back into the water and said to the beautiful stranger, 'Sorry, this is crazy, but I think God just told me I'm going to marry you.'

Shocked, the stranger said, 'That's odd. I think God told me the same, but I dismissed it as my mind playing tricks on me.'

They fell in love and lived happily ever after.

Part 3
TRUE LOVE

In relationship with yourself

The way you treat yourself matters. It feeds into your sense of self-worth and self-esteem. Your perception of your value ultimately informs the decisions you make for yourself. Vendors of high-end face cream and silk pillowcases would have you believe that self-care is reserved for the wealthy, but that's not true. Try this.

1 If you're staying somewhere for more than one night, unpack your stuff.

2 If you've been given a delivery slot between 2 and 3 p.m., plan to be home from 1 to 4 p.m.

3 Overwhelmed by your inbox? <Crtl + a> then <del>. If it's that important, they'll follow up.

4 Turn off read receipts on WhatsApp.

5 Spend five minutes a day in quiet meditation listening to God and you can't help but be changed for the better (from my vicar, the Revd Tim Stilwell).

6 When it comes to food, don't believe the hype that, left to your own devices, you'd guzzle chocolate and pick 'n' mix all day. Truly listen to your body and feed it the nourishing food it craves, with the occasional treat (from Deborah Frances-White, 2018).

7 Doing something today you'll be grateful for tomorrow applies particularly when you feel low and you're going to bed. Brush your teeth, remove your make-up, moisturize or whatever else is part of your routine. Tomorrow morning you will be grateful.

8 'Help me' are the most powerful words you can say.

9 If you find yourself with some spare money – a fiver you found on the street, a bonus you weren't expecting or a tax rebate you hadn't planned for – give it away if you possibly can. Their gain is not your loss. Their gain is your gain.

10 You don't need to be the banker in Monopoly, in charge of the remote, chief navigator for the road trip or deciding on the seating plan. Life is more relaxing when you relinquish control.

11 Accept gifts like a child. I've never heard my three-year-old nephew say, 'I can't take this, it's too much' or 'I really don't deserve this'. Be more Leo. Snap up that gift with glee and gratitude. Same rule applies to compliments.

12 You'll never feel lonely at the top if you do your best to take others there with you.

13 If it's 45 minutes on the train or 70 minutes to walk, factor in the extra 25 minutes and walk.

14 You don't have to be 'with child' to appreciate just how comfy a pregnancy pillow is.

15 There is no problem alcohol will make better in the long term. If you're feeling low, take a break from boozing.

16 Don't save things for 'best'. Use the fancy shampoo, burn the candle, take the tags off, make the effort. There's no such thing as best china. Today is a special occasion.

17 Detox from your phone and social media every now and again. It'll feel like coming up for air.

18 Know the difference between perseverance and perfectionism. Yes, you want to finish the run/exercise class/task/book, but every now and again it's more productive and character-building to give up. Let yourself.

19 Even if you see a work email out of hours, wait until you clock back in to reply.

20 The Bible/God really will comfort you if you allow them to. Invite them in and see what can happen.

In relationship with your friends

A quick search of the word 'love' on my WhatsApp showed that in the last week, I have had messages from 12 different people telling me they're sending their love, four directly addressing me as 'love' or 'my love' and five people who said the words: 'I love you'. I've dated none of them. These are people who care about me deeply, who are committed to investing in my life, affirming me, championing me, challenging me and encouraging me when I need it.

If true love is patient, kind, doesn't boast, isn't self-seeking, protects, trusts, hopes, always perseveres (1 Corinthians 13.4–8), then I've seen it modelled through my friendships more than anywhere else.

Maybe true love is the time Alex, knowing I don't drink alcohol, checked if she could use red wine vinegar in a recipe. Maybe it's the flowers sitting on my counter that Harri arranged from all the girls when I'd had a tough week. Maybe it's Emma, sending me links to cosy cardigans because she knew I loved hers and it was out of stock. Or maybe it's the time she researched the cost of a stint in The Priory's rehab facility when she could see my drug use was getting out of control. Maybe it's a care package from Tessa, brownies from Lizzie, tulips from Tim, a card from Clare, a voice note from Rachel; maybe it's a hug, a knowing smile, an in-joke, a home-cooked meal.

God has been quicker to answer my prayer for good friends than he ever has been for romance. Maybe that's because he knows what I need. I was two weeks sober and had been back at church for a week and a half when my friend Anna moved out of our Paris apartment to come home to London. I had a great group of friends in Paris. They were fun and supportive and kind, but none of them Christian. I prayed that I would make a Christian friend. Anna's room stayed empty for weeks while the landlord dragged his heels finding a replacement. With him, I sat through so many interviews that in the end I gave up and told him to pick whoever he liked. Another week or so went by and he said he'd found someone perfect. He insisted I meet her before she moved in. I arranged a quick coffee with her in Bastille before heading for lunch with a friend. She was fine. She would do.

True love

She moved in on a Saturday and went straight out to a bar before I could say hi. On the Sunday morning I knocked on her door and welcomed her to the flat. She had forgotten about the French's obsession with not opening their shops on Sundays (and often Mondays too) so hadn't stocked up on food before Carrefour closed on Saturday night. I offered to make her fajitas. I said I was heading out for the afternoon but would knock for her at 7ish when I was back. I left and went to church. When I got there, she was sitting two rows in front of me. I couldn't believe it. The service ended and she made a dash for it before I could corner her. I called her on my way home and asked where she'd been. She sheepishly confessed, 'Church,' sounding like she was concerned she was about to be thrown to the lions. I told her I'd been sitting behind her and that I'd booked a table at my favourite restaurant in the Marais. That night, we sat for hours together on the terrace. We ate and laughed and formed the foundations of a friendship I would come to treasure.

Katie became my confidante, my research buddy when there was some biblical concept I didn't understand, my rock. When she got married, I read a prayer in the service. She tells me she loves me every time I speak to her.

When I moved back to London, I prayed for Christian friends again. I was heading back to a city that had staged my cocaine-fuelled downfall. I knew more drug dealers in London than Christians. Katie knew a girl from university who lived in London and was active in her church. She put us in touch.

One of my old school friends had converted in the years I'd been away and she kindly took me along to her church: Hillsong in Tottenham Court Road. I also tried to reach out to Katie's recommended Christian but she seemed busy and we couldn't find a date that worked to meet up. I gave up and resigned myself to the bright lights and hipster crowds of Hillsong. I told Katie my decision but she wouldn't have it. She insisted I meet her friend, saying she just felt it was important.

Under strict instructions, I persevered and set up a coffee and church visit with this woman in West London. Lydia took me to St Dionis Church in Parsons Green. She introduced me to her friends and invited me to join the life group she ran. St Dionis felt like home and it still is today. Her friends became my friends and the wisdom and anecdotes from that group are laced through this book. The life group she ran cooked for me for months on end when my mental health took a dip while I was running the first Recovery Course. They clubbed together to pay for me to have therapy sessions. They dropped hot chocolate, candles and cards through my door. They prayed for me constantly. I hadn't known love like it.

I hear people talk about their partners in the most beautiful terms. 'Someone to laugh with you, and when you don't feel like laughing they stop to find out why'. 'Someone to do nothing with'. 'Someone to wipe away your tears'. 'Share your dreams'. 'Cheer you on'. 'Talk you up to strangers'. 'Keep you grounded'. 'Accept you with your flaws'. 'Pray for you, petition for you, hope for you when you're too weak to hope for yourself'. I've never been with a partner who can do those things as well as my friends. I don't know what kind of supernatural boyfriend could live up to the precedent they have set.

Maybe it's time to stop looking for a partner who is also my best friend and start appreciating my best friends. Maybe it's time to stop feeling bereft of true love and realize I already experience it. Every day.

In relationship with your family

The love of a family

If my family were a shape, it would be a straight-up square: me, my sister, my parents. But there are triangles, inverse triangles, rectangles, hexagons, stars, trees, big squiggles, lines and just dots. I want to tell you that a family is where you get unconditional love; it's where you are most known and most secure and that's what it should be. But I've worked with too many people on the Recovery Course to know that isn't everyone's story. If you have been consistently supported, encouraged and loved by yours, it's time to put a message on your family WhatsApp to say thank you. Because, this side of heaven, you will never know the momentous advantage this has given you in your life. A friend of mine, who's a teacher, said the children with parents who read with them before the age of three are the ones who do well in school. Something a lot of people would consider to be a small, simple thing at a very young age makes all the difference. Positive attention has a monumental influence on people.

Having a dysfunctional family is a risk factor for later antisocial behaviour, the development of addictions, eating disorders, bipolar disorder and that list doesn't end there. Studies have shown that a dysfunctional family can lead to more anxiety around dating and less dating advancement in young adults.

You didn't get to choose the shape of your family and the components in it. You may fall in the 'WhatsApp the family to say thank you' camp or you could be in the other. But unfortunately, that is generally out of your control. What is in your control is the family you create for yourself and the family member you set yourself up to be for others. That can be with your own nuclear family, your partner and children. It could be with someone else's family, your nieces and nephews or the family that lives across the road from you, or that of your godchildren. It could be the family environment you create with those at your church.

I am blessed to have the family I have. My parents are unfailingly supportive, they tell me often they are proud of me and get excited about the projects I'm working on. My sister is my best friend. She's hilarious and quick-witted and kind but absolutely brutal and one of the few people I can trust to pull no punches when I ask for her opinion. I've always known that, no matter what I did, they would be there. It's the most tangible example I have of unconditional love. I could commit a crime, go to prison for 20 years and at the 19-year mark, my parents and sister would still be visiting me. I can't say that's guaranteed for all my friends. Family love, when done right, does not waver or change. It is committed and consistent even under the most dreadful of circumstances.

Do you have that same level of commitment to your church family? Would you continue to visit someone for years on end if that person was in prison but still part of your church? What about when someone's bereaved? Three months after, when the shock has passed, are you still checking in? Still praying? Still cooking to help out? What about six months or a year? What about three years on? The pain may no longer be acute but it will still be there. Can you commit to consistency well after the novelty's worn off? When it stops being fun or exciting or adrenaline-fuelled crisis management?

During 2020's coronavirus pandemic, I started calling a woman who lived down the road from my church. She's 90 and had a swarm of people from the Neighbourhood Watch all buzzing round offering her shopping and conversation and friendship in the loneliness of isolation. By week six, she told me I was the only person who still called. That's where the church can be different.

Here's a fresh take on 1 Corinthians 13.4–8: Love is boring. Love is persistent. Love is tiring. Love is picking up the phone when you'd rather stick on the TV. Love is getting up, dressing up and showing up. Love is enduring. Love is showing that, no matter what someone does, you're not going anywhere. Love is waiting for someone to feel better. Love is sitting in silence. Love is a choice we should make every day. Because Jesus made it for us.

You can't do this for everyone. You can't phone everyone every day; you need to take self-care and boundaries seriously in order to love well. But when a church family comes together with this attitude, it is unstoppable. It is a force to be reckoned with. It counteracts the damaging effect of a dysfunctional biological family. I don't say that as a flippant Christian spiritual statement. It is recognized among researchers that church attendance is a protective factor against developing addiction. Church is powerful.

Turning church into family

For single people, finding family in church is vital. But at the moment we are often missing the mark. In the Single Friendly Church survey (2012), 37 per cent of people felt the Church doesn't treat single people as family members. One of the respondents said: 'When I look around the church on Christmas Day, everyone seems to be with their blood family in church, at which point I no longer feel that the church is my family.'

Forming a family from your church community is hard work. It requires action. No one likes that time of first getting to know someone. In the first few weeks I lived in my house at uni, I remember hating this adjustment period. There was a girl we had found by advertising who had moved in with the existing group of five of us. She was fun and beautiful and, according to her Facebook profile, enjoyed fancy dress a lot. Both our rooms were on the ground floor off the kitchen. I remember wanting to go to the kitchen to have a cigarette out of the back door but I could hear her moving around in there. I dreaded walking in. Not because I didn't like her, but because I didn't know her. I was desperate for that moment when we didn't make small talk but just had things to say to each other; when we had pushed through the awkward. And then at some point, without realizing it, we did.

There is a set amount of time you have to be in someone's company before you are no longer in small-talk territory. It may not feel like it, but you can push through with absolutely anyone. With some people it will take 15 minutes, others 60 hours. But if it's still awkward, just know that every effort, every minute, every bit of chit-chat is in aid of the moment when you are past it. You have to push through the awkward. Once you get there – once you know someone – that's when you start enjoying that person's company; when you start to *really* get to know one another and how best you can support each other. That's when you're building family and that's what church should feel like.

A new vision for community

What became apparent through the research and interviews for this book was that we need to rethink the way we do community. If we want to encourage people that there's nothing wrong with staying single and it's an equal state to being married, then we need to put a framework in place whereby someone can be on their own but still have companionship.

Bella said: 'I think Western culture at large must change so as to be more community-focused and welcoming towards single people of all ages, in both philosophical and practical terms. This could be by comprehending better what we lack emotionally and socially in our lives, assisting unwell single people and making housing more affordable.'

There are ways the Church – as a body of people rather than just an individual – can step in here and make a real difference to people's lives.

Clare, the friend of mine who left London to foster children and has done so as a single woman said: 'The thing that would actually support me most would be having a few people who will come and stay the night here with the children to give me a night off. People often want to give meals or pray or give money. But investing time in someone to the extent that you would come into their home and give them a break is rare but so valuable.'

The more I thought about this, the more it occurred to me that, in modern society, we've forgotten how to sacrifice in order to live well in a group. We talk so much about maintaining boundaries that we're boxing ourselves in inside them. We've forgotten how to fearlessly and disruptively love.

A few months after I moved into my flat, I realized that my neighbours were Christian; I spotted them through the window hosting a book club, which, on closer inspection, turned out to be a Bible study. I had Zac and Zoe over for a cup of tea and Zac, who turned out to lead Every Day Church in Clapham, said something that really stuck with me: 'There's a guy in our church who says we've started to confuse entertainment with hospitality. Entertainment is nice: you clean the house, you cook something special, you offer someone a drink when they come in. But hospitality is leaving the door on the latch; having someone come and crash on the sofa or stay for dinner but it's only pasta with what's left in the cupboard. It's leaving them to put their own dish in the dishwasher. Entertainment is inviting someone in to watch a performance. Hospitality is inviting someone into your family.'

James and Sophia feel passionately about this model of living and are planning to set up a community house, with two couples and six single people all living as one household unit. A family with companionship – somewhere where people can have a bad day but not in isolation. To the untrained ear it may sound like a hippy commune but I believe there's something in it.

I currently live on my own. I know I have become comfortable not having to adapt to others. If I put something down, it's still there the next day. I can use the living room for an online Pilates class without checking with anyone else first. I can play my music or watch the TV with no one to fight for the remote. But on the flipside, I don't like the emptiness, the quiet, not being able to turn to someone and make a joke about what I'm watching. I don't like eating meals on the sofa by myself. So, I decided to open up my house. I arranged for access to keys for ten people who lived within walking distance, stocked up on tea and biscuits and offered for anyone to come and hang out. Whether I'm home or not, they can use the space for work, for prayer or to relax. I showed people where the kettle, fridge and snack cupboard were and I left them to make themselves at home. I didn't serve anyone. And people started coming.

I don't get to choose what goes on the TV all the time any more. Sometimes someone will finish the milk or leave the toilet seat up or fill the bin to the top and expect me to take it out. Sometimes I may feel like some alone-time but someone else is round. I had always expected to have to compromise on those things but previously only thought it would be worth it in exchange for a relationship. But what I've learned is, if I'm willing to relinquish control and some comfort, what I get back is the everyday companionship I would otherwise miss out on. When I dropped the boundaries I'd spent so long insisting were key for my mental health, I found a depth of community that was far more deeply satisfying. This is what community looks like. It's annoying and intrusive and not always in line with your mood. It's not synced up with your diary and it's not always convenient. But this is how I allowed myself to become truly known; how I've learned to share my life with people; how I get daily companionship.

This is love.

Community in the Church: solutions not problems

1 Check with single people what their plan is for Christmas/Easter and make sure everyone is welcomed in somewhere.

2 Don't put pressure on people to pair up. Christian single people – in fact, the majority of single people full stop – do not need to feel additional pressure to find a relationship. In my experience they already pile enough of that on themselves.

3 Stop viewing life as a linear progression through modes, with some further along than others. Life's trajectory doesn't have to be single > dating > married > house > children.

4 Don't put the burden of the gender imbalance in your church back on the women. Find new ways to invite in and relate to men.

5 Be mindful of how many family and couple references you have in your sermons. Ask single people for their thoughts.

6 Listen without always offering an answer.

7 Rethink how you offer community. If single people in your church don't have families they're friends with, where they can just rock up unannounced and get stuck into family life, help them develop friendships to find those relationships.

8 Address the difficulties of being single and dating. Address it in prayer, ask people how they are, give sermons on it. Don't try to tackle the 'problem of being single' and encourage everyone to get married, but instead recognize there are challenges associated with being single and dating, and address those.

9 Offer to introduce people you know. Don't just assume your friends wouldn't get on. Get all the single people you know in a room together often.

10 'Empathy, and sitting in the pain, naming it, is far more valuable than false comfort and clichéd advice.' *Party of One* – Joy Beth Smith (2018).

11 Treat everyone the same regardless of whether they are single-never-married, married, divorced or widowed. Ensure your leadership positions and PCC have a mix of all stages of life.

12 Host events that are for your single people. If you don't have many, make an effort to connect with other churches and combine groups. Don't call them 'singles events' – just non-pressurized environments where people who have common interests can meet – catchy title, eh?

13 Make sure you have single people speaking from the front as role models. It's not just married couples who can plant a church or run a ministry or speak at a conference.

14 Stop highlighting that someone's married unless it is relevant (there are a number of times when it is – but ask yourself the question).

15 Check in when people are ill. Make sure someone is bringing them soup, buying them magazines, sending them Netflix recommendations and, if they are really unwell, even running their baths, cooking their food, transporting them places and helping them dress. That is family.

In relationship with Christ

I've got this friend. They're never late; just like clockwork, always there. They celebrate with me, laugh with me, cry with me. They're the first person I speak to when I wake up. I tell them about my worries, fears, aspirations and even the dark, horrible thoughts in the deepest crevices of my mind. They listen; they don't judge. They step in from time to time to offer comfort and encouragement or sometimes they just hear me out.

But we haven't always been so close. There was a time when I didn't want the friendship. I was busy having fun and they didn't approve so I pushed them away. I shut the door and blocked them out. I didn't want them there, highlighting my flaws. But they're still there.

Imagine you have a friend who just does not leave you. It doesn't matter what you do, they're still there. For better, for worse, there is no cross word or misjudged action that can make them go. They know you at your absolute worst. They know the depraved actions, desperate decisions and evil thoughts that have crossed your mind. They've seen you snap, shout, judge, gossip, show off, give the finger to other drivers. But they're still there.

They stay nearby while you drink yourself to oblivion, walk with you down dark alleys to meet your dealer, watch while you flirt with strangers whose names you'll never remember. But they're still there. They make sure you get home OK; they keep an eye on you to make sure you don't overdose or choke on your own vomit. Their presence makes you feel guilty. You suspect their faithful guardianship is veiled with judgement. Why wouldn't they judge you? You judge yourself. You lash out at them, laugh at them with other friends, make jokes at their expense when they're in earshot. But they're still there. They absorb it, knowing that if you were thinking straight, you'd never say it. It hurts, but they don't stop loving you.

In times of realization, you allow them in. They pull you close and wrap their arms around you in those brief windows of clarity. They cry with you while you struggle to come to terms with the pain. They push the lid of the toilet down and perch there while you sit on the floor of the shower and cry. Then you shut them back out again, unable to cope with the reality you've created. But they're still there.

They don't always reply when you speak to them. They don't intervene or even tell you off. They wouldn't choose to be in those places, but they follow you there anyway. They know you need them. They don't enjoy it. It hurts and it's disappointing and their heart breaks. But they're still there. Always there. Just loving you. For better, for worse. Patiently waiting for the penny to drop. For you to realize there is no shadow too dark or rabbit hole too cavernous or place too desperate to stop them following you down there. You can't put them off deeply loving you, no matter how hard you try. They will kick down doors, cross borders, intercede, carefully strategize and go to war for you. They will mobilize armies. But more difficult than all that, they wait. They sit patiently by your side and wait while you reject them and hit self-destruct again. But they're still there. Waiting for you to realize how much they value you and how much you should value yourself.

When you finally give in, when you finally accept it, when you finally turn back to look through the wreck of the life you've left behind you, they're still there. They kneel with you on the floor and help you sort through the pieces. They hand you bricks while you try to relay the foundations. It's still hard but it's different this time. They celebrate every small win with you. They tell you they're proud of you. They call other friends and get them to rally round; they help you get a team.

They are your biggest champion, your biggest supporter. They still see your faults, but they're different now. They talk through them with you, help you make a plan to work it out. You still mess up. But they're still there. They never step back and decide their work is done. They never say that, now you're on your feet, you don't need them any more. They walk with you, they laugh with you, they still cry with you from time to time.

Sometimes they point you to a shadow, show you a door that needs kicking down or someone who needs their hair holding back. Sometimes they show you how you can help. How you can help someone else realize how loved they are. How you can help the penny to drop. But they never send you in there on your own. They check the room before they send you in; stand by your side so you can burst through the door together. When it gets messy and you think for a second you could be alone, you look back but they're still there. Always there.

And finally . . .

At the end of your life, you will never wish you'd loved less. Sometimes it can feel painful. You can feel like battening down the hatches, cocooning yourself away and giving up. You can put up walls and keep your guard high. But if Jericho's anything to go by, God knows how to break down walls. The Spirit knows what you need. Sometimes your job is to silence your head.

I want your takeaway to be that of hope. Not the hope that you'll find your perfect partner. The fact is that, even if you do, there is no perfect. There will be moments of elation, but the reality is that being in a relationship is just as challenging as being single – in different ways. The hope I would like you to take away is that God has a plan for you. He loves and backs you. And whatever he has laid ahead of you, you won't regret it. It will be difficult. It will have challenges, but you'll be proud you walked it.

A friend of mine said something just before she gave birth to her fourth child, which has always stuck with me. In the anxiousness and anticipation of going into labour, she said, 'What if God is about to abundantly bless me?' What if he is? What if he's about to answer prayers you didn't even know you had? What if you're so focused on how things could go wrong or deviate from *your* plan that you're missing the massive gifts in front of you right now?

Another wise friend recently told me, 'If you can't see how God is good in a situation, he's not done working.' The fact is, God is not working for your happiness. Happiness is shallow and fleeting and vapid and self-focused. The secret of life is not to find happiness. And if it were, you won't suddenly find it once you're in a relationship. God's goal for you is abundant life, not a perfect life. He is working towards your fulfilment, peace and joy (which is not the same as happiness). Sometimes the most poignant moments in your life, the ones you're most grateful for, will be the sad ones. This book was written when I was low. At times it's all I've been able to do to drag myself over to my laptop and type. But that doesn't mean I won't look back on it with fondness. It is still a pivotal memory for me and one I am grateful for.

When the pain hits and the hard times come (and they will, single or in a relationship), I fight to remind myself that God's not the enemy. He's not the source of the problem but he is the source of the solution.

Stay as close to God as you possibly can through everything. It's like running a gauntlet. The enemy is going to throw loads at you, sometimes daily: heartbreak, longing, bereavement, health troubles, financial worries. Sometimes the things he throws will even look good: relationships, a pay rise, a new car, smoking hot looks. But if you can take these things and still keep your sights firmly on God, you have won. This doesn't mean life will be easy and the things will stop being thrown, but you will have the armour to stay standing (Ephesians 6.10–18) and that's all we're called to do. Stay standing as close to him as possible.

Don't let something that is supposed to be good – a relationship or the hope for one – become the thing that knocks you down and away from God. It should never become an idol, or worse an addiction. If you can feel that it has, challenge it and refocus. God's promises are secure and he is clear when he says: 'Don't panic. I'm with you. There's no need to fear for I'm your God. I'll give you strength. I'll help you. I'll hold you steady, keep a firm grip on you' (Isaiah 41.10, MSG). Choose to stay close to God even when it feels too much. It's in those moments that you'll recognize the true love.

Know that whether you are in a relationship or not, you are never alone. You are never out of options. Never left to fend for yourself. What I love about Jesus is that when he was backed into a corner and given two choices, neither of which were ideal, he always found secret option C. He didn't condemn or release the adulterous woman (John 8.1–11). He didn't condone or reject the paying of taxes (Matthew 22.15–22). He was never actually between a rock and a hard place despite the best attempts of his enemies. You've got that ingenuity, that foresight, that wisdom on your side. Working for you. Don't forget it.

Next, you need to know your identity isn't in your relationship status. It's also not in your job or your style or the area you live in or your political opinions or the church you go to. If you place your identity and value in transient, changeable things, you will never feel stable and secure. You are also not waiting for anything. You are not perched on the blocks listening out for the starting pistol. The race began ages ago; life started. You need to mobilize. It's time to get working for God's mission in your life.

What you are being called to is more than marriage. Marriage may be on your journey but it's not your destination. There's no way God saw you and thought, 'This person's exclusive value to me is as a husband/wife to someone else.' There is something kingdom-building in your path and that's what you're working towards. If God has someone for you, it's because you can achieve more for him together.

If you decide to date, that's great. But don't date because you don't feel loved. Everything you do should be from a position of understanding how loved you are. That grounding will help you make decisions that honour yourself and those around you. Just in case you're not sure, it is impossible for me to describe the depth of love God feels for you. Absolutely nothing will stop him loving you (Romans 8.38–39), even if you don't believe that to be true. God's love is profound and if you let it, it can define you; it can be your identity. If everyone on earth started from a real understanding of God's love for them, there would be no need for heaven. It is so inspiring and pivotal and monumental that it stirs a passion in you that can't be replicated. This isn't love that gives you tummy butterflies, it's love that gives you fire in your belly. You can't earn it, you can't earn more; you also can't do anything to shake it off. It is not based on your actions. He loves you because of who he is, not because of who you are. You won't be able to find this level of love in a person, so don't even try. Don't try to find a partner who can match the depth and intensity of God. You won't.

Once you get how loved you are, it's time to pay it forward. Show that love to God, your neighbours, your friends, your church, your leaders, your family, the crazy woman who always sits next to you on the bus, the guy behind the counter at the petrol station, the person who collects your bins on a Tuesday and, if it's part of your story, your husband/wife. Focus on the time you spend with the people you love, the times you share with them and the opportunities to love them well. This is your treasure.

It's fine to date, it's fine for it to be fun, it's fine for it to be painful at times, but it's not fine for it to pull you away from God. Don't forget who he is; that he doesn't change even when your circumstances do. That the love he has for you will never be rivalled, no matter how many online dating profiles you sift through.

With all that in mind, this is my prayer for you:

I pray that you settle. That you settle for too short or too tall. For not enough money or a student without a 'proper job'. For someone who doesn't own a home and probably never will. For someone who doesn't speak any other languages and can't play an instrument. For someone who's not been Christian long enough or is 'too Christian'. For someone who's never had sex or for someone who's had too much sex. For someone whose past isn't squeaky clean. For someone whose mum is too present in their life or for someone who never knew their dad. For someone who doesn't quite get your jokes on the first date and doesn't actually find *The Office* that funny. For someone who would take a while to warm up if you introduced them to your friends. For someone who is not your type. For someone you wouldn't usually go for. For someone who doesn't tick all your boxes.

I pray that you never feel forced to compromise on connection but are open to God showing it to you in places you didn't expect. That you will never settle for someone you don't care for deeply, because 'you should'. Or for someone who isn't kind. Or for someone who isn't gracious and generous. Or for someone who doesn't freely give you their time. Or for someone who doesn't recognize the importance of your spiritual life and champion it above all else. I pray that God will give you the tools to identify when you have met a teammate, who will dream with you and complement you as you achieve what he set out for you to achieve.

I pray that, if you are longing to meet someone, you do. I pray that you meet a best friend, so you don't need a partner as your primary companion. I pray that you can join or build an amazing church community, so you don't need a partner to be your only support. I pray that you are deeply connected with your Saviour, so you don't need a partner to rescue you. I pray that, as you survey your incredible network of connections and the relationships that keep you afloat, you will see a partner as an enhancement, not an essential.

If you don't want to meet someone, I pray that you will be recognized as the fully formed, whole, competent and valuable person you are. I pray every penny you spend on single-occupancy rates is a piece of treasure stored up for you in heaven. I pray that you will embrace and appreciate the perks of being single and, with your unanchored life, you will move mountains for God.

I pray that this will spark conversations in churches. That leaders will look around and ask themselves if they are doing enough to reinforce the importance of each individual and not each couple. I pray that no one will use the phrase 'pairs and spares' again. I pray that no person will ever be made to feel like a spare part, a gap-filler, a loose end in God's house, but that it will be the place where they feel most welcome and most valued.

I pray that single people remember this is fun. That this isn't a lonely, bitter period of pain and rejection. That this isn't being left on the shelf. That this is a freedom others long for. That the heartbreak and anguish and uncertainty are developing character in us that we would never trade, even if the journey there is tough. I pray that we can meet new people. That we can flirt. That we can choose where we go and when and what we do and how much we spend on it. I pray that we start dancing on tables. Literally dancing on tables. Because we can. Because there's no baby at home or partner who's waiting up. If that's in the future, we can jump down off the trestle when the time comes.

But for now, we are free to dance on the _____ing tables.

Acknowledgements

I would be remiss if I didn't start at the top. I've got to thank God, who I believe gave me the opportunity to write this and then systematically presented me with wise people saying wise things to fill its pages.

Elizabeth Neep, the editor who commissioned and worked with me on this book. I can't imagine going through the process with anyone else. Your updates, edits and comments have improved this book immeasurably. Thanks for handling it with such wisdom and sensitivity. Thanks also to Alexa Tewkesbury, who copy-edited this book and negotiated a perfect balance between proper English and the incorrect grammar to which I had grown attached. Thank you for the respect you've shown to both my tone and your standards. For your next career, I suggest hostage negotiations or something at the UN. And thanks to the SPCK marketing department and the designers who put together the dreamiest of all the dreamy book covers.

Next, my family, Mum, Dad, Cathie, Nathan, Leo and Winnie. I don't underestimate how bizarre it is when people you're related to write about their love life. Sorry you had to sit through it but thank you for your unwavering support, declarations of pride and invaluable proofreading. I haven't put it on our family WhatsApp yet, but I am so grateful for you all.

In recent years I have been blessed with a number of incredible mentors, both official and unofficial. Desi, my sponsor S, Jo and Tim, thank you for your guidance, both spiritual and personal, as I navigated through some of the challenges detailed in this book. I consider your involvement in my life to be a gift from God.

Emmanuelle, I don't know if you'll ever read this. Do therapists read their clients' books? But you should know that you changed my life. Over seven years, you guided me through hangovers and comedowns, encouraged me to go to meetings, helped me unpick my past and hope for the future. You cheer me on without hesitation and it means the world to me. I aspire to be the person you believe me to be.

George H, would either of us be authors if it hadn't been for that team dinner at Pizza Express? I can still hear Sophie saying, 'Oh no, only one of you is going to get published and then it's going to be really awkward.' I thank God she hasn't got the gift of the prophetic.

Thanks also go to Ali M – who once told me not to get it right, but to get it written. Advice I remind myself of regularly.

Shlads; Sam, Tim, Lizzie, Meriel and Angus. My focus group, my pick-me-up, my cheerleaders, my friends. What would this book be without our dinners, WhatsApp group and long, languishing conversations?

Emma, Alex, Harri, Lou, Robs and Ross, what did I do to deserve such encouraging friends? Thanks for the lockdown puzzles, book recommendations, documentaries and decades of memories. I am for ever grateful that I didn't chase you away in my drug-taking years. Aaron, who brings me ice-cream every time I get dumped. Barney, whose encyclopaedic knowledge of *The Office* and general quick wit always keeps me on my toes. Jessie, for suggesting someone write a book along these lines and planting a seed.

Rachel and Lucy C, these pages are dripping with your wisdom and encouragement. The links you send me, the screengrabs, the times you just voice-note me to say you're praying are so treasured.

Tess, I don't know when you'll read this and hopefully by then I will have said it to you in person: you are amazing. Your consistency as a friend is unparalleled. Over the months when I was writing this book, you have known what I needed better than I have myself. You never got bored with supporting me. You just kept showing up. I love you for that (and for many other things).

Clare, I wrote the first draft introduction for this book in a coffee shop down at the beach while you worked Parkrun. When you came back, you read through it and laughed so loud we got funny looks in the shop. It was the encouragement I needed to push on with the project. I love that we make each other laugh out loud and I don't care who can hear. You don't like praise and you hear it a lot – but you, and the way you care for others, are truly an inspiration.

To all the men I've loved before – thank you for generously allowing me to use our experiences, both good and bad, in this book. Thank you for every kind word, laugh, date, message, prayer, book, song, dance and meal we shared that made me feel so special. Every moment helped me learn something more about myself.

And finally, but most importantly, to every single person who replied to a shout-out I put on social media, every person who replied to my

Acknowledgements

WhatsApp requests, agreed to have coffee with me or participated in a focus group: you have made this book what it is. The anecdotes and opinions have had me laughing and crying for months. This book is a true collaboration. Hatty, Ramsey, Laura, Lucy, Ruth, Clare, Barney, Andrew, Phoebe, Titi, Lulu, Janine, Jen, Isabella, Charlotte, Norris, Lord John, Wesley, Clayton, Robin, Rory, Andrew, Jess L, Ali G (how have I just realized your name abbreviates to that?!), Claire, Uncle Milton, Sam S, Steve, Justin, David and Zac – without you, my editor would have received a few disjointed ideas submitted on the back of a tear-stained napkin.

Bibliography

After Life (2019) Netflix (available online at: <https://netflix.com/gb/title/80998491>).

Allberry, Sam (2019) *7 Myths About Singleness* (Wheaton, Illinois: Crossway Books).

Ansari, Aziz (2015) *Modern Romance* (London: Allen Lane).

Atwood, Margaret (1985) *The Handmaid's Tale* (Toronto: McClelland and Stewart).

Augustine Fellowship (1985) '40 questions for self-diagnosis', 1985 (available online at: <https://slaafws.org/download/core-files/The_40_Questions_of_SLAA.pdf>,accessed 2020).

Beattie, Melody (2018) *Codependent No More: How to stop controlling others and start caring for yourself* (Center City, Minnesota: Hazelden FIRM).

Comer, John Mark (2017) *God Has a Name* (Grand Rapids, Michigan: Zondervan Trade).

EvFree Fullerton Church (2013) *Sex, Love & God Podcast* (available online at: <https://podcasts.apple.com/gb/podcast/evfree-fullerton-sex-love-and-god-podcast/id722950415>).

Falango, Mark (2012) 'Love addiction self-assessment', 2012 (available online at: <http://markfalango. com/wp-content/uploads/2012/05/lasa.pdf>, accessed 2020).

Fisher, H. E., Brown, L. L., Aron, A., Strong, G. and Mashek, D. (2010) 'Reward, addiction, and emotion regulation systems associated with rejection in love', *Journal of Neurophysiology*, 104(1): 51–60.

Fisher, H. E., Xu X., Aron, A. and Brown, L. L. (2016) 'Intense, passionate, romantic love: A natural addiction? How the fields that investigate romance and substance abuse can inform each other', *Frontiers in Psychology*, 7: 687.

Fisher, H. E. (2017) *Anatomy of Love: A natural history of mating, marriage, and why we stray* (New York: W. W. Norton & Company).

Foster, Richard (1985) *Money, Sex and Power* (London: Hodder & Stoughton).

Bibliography

Frances-White, Deborah (2018) *The Guilty Feminist* (London: Virago).

Griffin-Shelley, E. (1997) *Sex and Love: Addiction, treatment, and recovery* (Santa Barbara, California: Praeger).

Harris, Joshua (1997) *I Kissed Dating Goodbye* (Colorado Springs, Colorado: Multnomah Press).

Harris, Joshua (2018) *I Survived I Kissed Dating Goodbye* (available online at: <https://youtube.com/watch?v=ybYTkkQJw_M>).

Hsu, Al (1998) *The Single Issue* (Leicester: IVP).

Lexico.com (available online at: <https://lexico.com/definition/schrodinger%27s_cat>).

makerswomen on Instagram (2019) (available online at: <https://instagram.com/p/BxAPCN5F9Sl/?igshid=wkfmsii7e01c>).

Mellody, Pia (2003) *Facing Love Addiction: Giving yourself the power to change the way you love* (San Francisco, California: HarperOne).

Meloy, J. R. and Fisher, H. (2005) 'Some thoughts on the neurobiology of stalking', *Journal of Forensic Sciences*, 50(6): 1–9.

Reynaud, M., Karila, L., Blecha, L. and Benyamina, A. (2010) 'Is love passion an addictive disorder?', *The American Journal of Drug and Alcohol Abuse*, 36(5): 261–7.

Sanches M. and John, V. (2019) 'Treatment of love addiction: Current status and perspectives', *The European Journal of Psychiatry*, 33(1): 38–44.

Schwartz, Barry (2005) 'The paradox of choice', TED Talk at TEDGlobal 2005 (available online at: <https://ted.com/talks/barry_schwartz_the_paradox_of_choice>).

Sex and the City: The Movie (2008) New Line Cinema.

Sharma, Sonya (2008) *Women and Religion in the West: Challenging secularization* (Abingdon: Routledge).

Single Friendly Church (2012) 'Singleness in the UK Church' survey (available online at: <https://singlefriendlychurch.com/research/research>).

Smith, Joy Beth (2018) *Party of One: Truth, longing, and the subtle art of singleness* (Nashville, Tennessee: Thomas Nelson).

Snow White and the Seven Dwarfs (1937) Walt Disney Productions.

Steinbeck, John (1937) *Of Mice and Men* (New York City: Covici Friede).

Strauss, Neil (2007) *The Game* (London: Canongate Books).

Sussman, S. (2010) 'Love addiction: Definition, etiology, treatment', *Sexual Addiction & Compulsivity*, 17(1): 31–45.

Sussman, S. (2017) *Substance and Behavioral Addictions Concepts,Causes and Cures* (Cambridge: Cambridge University Press).

Bibliography

Sussman, S. (2020) *The Cambridge Handbook of Substance and Behavioral Addictions* (Cambridge: Cambridge University Press).

Sztainert, T. (2017) 'Gambling in the DSM and ICD', *Gambling Research Exchange Ontario* (available online at: <https://bit.ly/3nBu6Kr>, accessed: 2020).

Too Hot to Handle (2020) Netflix (available online at: <https://netflix.com/gb/title/80241027>).

Tyson, Jon (2018) 'Singleness', sermon at Church of the City New York, Sunday 15 April 2018 (available online at: <https://youtube.com/watch?v=AcN8sdGckF4>).

Ulvaeus, Björn ABBA (1976) 'Knowing Me, Knowing You'.

Verbi, Samuel (2014) 'There aren't enough men' HTB survey (available online at: <https://scripties.uba.uva.nl/download?fid=636083>).

Whitesnake (1987) 'Here I Go Again '87' from the 1987 album *Whitesnake*.

Windle, Lauren (2016) 'From adult Disney lovers to gluten-free singles: A week of dates from the UK's most niche dating sites', *The Sun* (2016) (available online at: <https://thesun.co.uk/living/1573921/from-adult-disney-lovers-to-gluten-free-singles-a-week-of-dates-from-the-uks-most-niche-dating-sites>).

Windle, Lauren (2018a) 'Could crying in the corner of a pub REALLY bag me a man? I put bonkers dating advice to the test', *The Sun* (available online at: <https://thesun.co.uk/fabulous/7774408/cry-in-pub-1950s-dating-techniques>).

Windle, Lauren (2018b) 'Lessons a drug addict can teach you', TEDx Talk at Surrey University, Saturday 3 March (available online at: <https://ted.com/talks/lauren_windle_lessons_a_drug_addict_can_teach_you>).

Windle, Lauren (2018c) 'We tried out Greggs' £15 four-course Valentine's Day meal for a first date – to see if love can blossom over a Sausage and Bean Melt', *The Sun* (available online at: <https://thesun.co.uk/fabulous/food/5533232/greggs-four-course-valentines-day-meal>).

Windle, Lauren (2019) 'Christian dating: In search of that Bible-study spark', *Church Times* (available online at: <https://churchtimes.co.uk/articles/2019/24-may/features/features/christian-dating-in-search-of-that-bible-study-spark>).

World Health Organization (2013) 'Global and regional estimates of violence against women' (available online at: <http://who.int/iris/bitstream/10665/85239/1/9789241564625_eng.pdf>).

Courses

Celebrate Recovery (information available at: <https://celebraterecovery.com>).

Recovery Course (information available at: <https://therecoverycourse.com>).

Steps Programme (information available at: <https://stepscourse.org/about>).

Information on and links to secular programmes are available on Lauren's website at: <https://laurenwindle.com/lauren-windle-addiction-recovery>.

WE HAVE A VISION OF A WORLD IN WHICH EVERYONE IS TRANSFORMED BY CHRISTIAN KNOWLEDGE

As well as being an award-winning publisher, SPCK is the oldest Anglican mission agency in the world.

Our mission is to lead the way in creating books and resources that help everyone to make sense of faith.

Will you partner with us to put good books into the hands of prisoners, great assemblies in front of schoolchildren and reach out to people who have not yet been touched by the Christian faith?

To donate, please visit www.spckpublishing.co.uk/donate or call our friendly fundraising team on 020 7592 3900.